Alice & Frosty

An American Adventure

Gail Kurrle Wilkinson

Written by Gail Kurrle Wilkinson

Alice & Frosty
An American Adventure

Alice & Frosty
Copyright 2010 Gail Wilkinson

THE IOWAN 📖 books

CEO....................Jim Slife
Publisher..............Polly Clark
Editing/Design......Nichole Kelderman

An Iowan Books Publication
300 Walnut Street - Suite 6
Des Moines, IA 50309
515.246.0402
www.Iowan.com

First Printing: March 2010
Printed in U.S.A.

A Gail Wilkinson Book
ISBN 9781934816141

Dedication

For BJ, Zach, Mitch and Shelby, and the bright, memorable, American adventure we're living.

Acknowledgement

All of the stories recounted in this book are true, with the exception of Frosty's hair catching on fire. Frosty's letters are his actual writings home from WWI.

Thanks to the many family members who contributed memories and encouragement to the making of this book. Special thanks to my mom and Alice's daughter, Greta Appleton Kurrle, for the illustrations, and my sister, also Alice and Frosty's granddaughter, editor Polly Clark. Thanks to the kids on the cover - my daughter, Shelby, and Ellie Niemann, and photographer Tracy Niemann.

Lastly, I'm grateful for my grandma, Alice, who recorded her hopes and history in colorful spiral notebooks, and spun many a great story on the front porch swing.

Contents

Twelve year old Alice perched on a stool in the hallway, the tips of her high-button shoes pecking the floor
like barnyard chickens. Her back ached from sitting lady-
like. Beside her in a proper chair sat her sister, Minnie, her
dress crisp and unwrinkled. Alice was suddenly aware
that her sweaty palms had clutched her Sunday dress into
bunches. Both girls eyed the bedroom door at the end of
the hall, Minnie with curiosity and Alice with the darting
eyes of a scared squirrel.

"Minnie," Alice whispered. "What is taking so long?
We have been waiting for hours!"

"It's only been a little while," Minnie replied. "Be pa-
tient."

"Min, I've been thinking, do you think the baby will be
red and wrinkly like the kittens when they're newborn?
Should I say she's pretty, even if she's not?"

An annoyed look flitted across Minnie's face and Alice
knew she'd said the wrong thing. "The new baby will be
beautiful, Alice," she scolded under her breath. "Be sure
to tell Ma she looks pretty too." Alice felt like she had a
biscuit lodged in her throat. She swallowed. It was hard

for her to say nice things to her new ma.

The bedroom door swung open. A neighbor lady, arms crossed, squinted at the pair. "Girls, you can come in now. Absolutely no loud talking or laughing." Alice surveyed the gatekeeper, her fuzzy gray bun reminding Alice of a kitten she'd just played with in the barn. Nervously, Alice started to giggle. Minnie glanced at her with alarm.

"Please, Al," Minnie whispered. "Be good." Alice nodded. Minnie was always right about being good. Minnie slipped her cool hand into her sister's and squeezed it as they tip-toed into the bedroom.

Ma was buried under a pile of quilts in the tall, four-poster bed. The girls barely recognized her. Her eyelids drooped and damp strands of hair clung to her pale face. "Ma!" Minnie cried, rushing to the bed. Alice, lingered by the door. Minnie touched her Mother's cheek and her eyes fluttered open. She smiled weakly. "Come closer, girls, and take a peek at the baby."

Alice just noticed the tiny baby between the quilts. She scooted to the foot of the bed and peered into the deep pile of bedding. A little pink head with wisps of black hair snuggled against Ma's arm. Alice could just see a tiny hand gripping the sheet.

Minnie picked up a brush from the nightstand and began to untangle Ma's matted hair. They chatted softly. The baby stretched one of her little fists and Alice scrambled onto the bed, excitedly gushing, "Hello little Evelyn!" Jostled, the baby began to cry, and Ma moaned.

"Alice!" said a harsh voice from the corner of the room. "You let that baby be! We can't have children clamoring all over that infant!" Alice slipped off the bed and bent her head to face Pa. She hadn't noticed him sitting in the darkness in the rocking chair. Now Pa was on his feet, and

Alice backed to the window like a cornered dog. "Oh Al," Minnie said, her eyes brimming with pity and disappointment. Ma's face pinched in annoyance.

All eyes in the room focused on Alice. With one deep gulp Alice dashed from the room, dropping a pillow embroidered in uneven pink script. It read, "Baby Crone, Born 1907. With love from Alice."

Alice ran through the parlor, past the kitchen and into the farmyard. Her tears stung her cheeks in the cold, spring air. When she reached the barn, she wrenched open the door. "I will not let them see me bawl like a baby," she said. Smells from the hay mound scratched her nose and she sneezed, startling a cat curled in one of the cow stalls. The tabby sauntered over and Alice dropped to the dirt floor, gathering her in a tight squeeze.

"Well, well," came a grown-up voice from the end of the barn. "If it isn't the kitty girl."

"Hi, Bernie," Alice murmured to her older brother.

Bernie walked out of the shadows, his tall, figure blocking the light. He wiped his hands with an old flannel rag. "So," he began, watching Alice from the corner of his eye. "Is the new baby as cute as a button?"

Alice thought about the question as the tabby batted at her pigtails. "Yes," she murmured. "She's very cute. She was snuggled in with Ma looking just like she belonged."

When you were born twelve years ago, all I remember is how fiercely you howled," teased Bernie.

"Sure, when I found out I had such a mean older brother," Alice replied, a smile tugging at her mouth.

Bernie pulled over a tin milking bucket and up-ended it for a stool. "Our family sure is growing," he said, once again putting the rag to work on his greasy hands.

Alice's face fell and a tear rolled down her cheek. "I

don't think Pa and Ma like me," she whispered. "No matter what I'm always the one that makes Ma grouchy and Pa mad!"

"Now Al, don't take it so hard. You know Ma hasn't felt well. And Pa is gruff with everyone these days. Ma's been laid up and two other little ones have been taking up all Pa's time."

"That's another thing, Bernie. Who ever heard of families living in two different houses like we do? As long as I can remember, it has been you and Min and I living on the other farm, and Ma and Pa and the little kids over here. It's like they don't even want us to live with them! Doesn't it seem odd to come over here and pretend we're in the same family? Sometimes I don't even think little Phoebe and Orville think of us as their sisters and brother. Now baby Evelyn might get to thinking we're just visitors too."

"Well, Al," Bernie said. "A family is what you make it. I reckon people can be in the same family and live in two places."

"The other kids tease me about it," Alice muttered. "They don't think it's right that Ma and Pa live at their own place. They say Ma doesn't like us."

Bernie reached down to stroke the tabby's tummy. "You're a smart girl, Al." Too old to let stories bother you, wouldn't you say?"

Alice shrugged. "Would it have been different if our real mother had lived?"

"I'm sure it would have been."

"Tell me about her, Bernie. I can't hardly remember her."

"My memory of her gets dimmer too," Bernie said. I'm eighteen years old now, but I was eleven when she died. "I still remember walking through town with her, back when they still had the wooden sidewalks. Her boots tap-tapped, real graceful like. She was so pretty that people turned their heads just to watch her pass. She wore her dark hair put up with shiny combs and she had a bright smile for everyone. Her eyes were brown as the richest coffee. As a matter of fact, I think you look quite a bit like her."

Alice blushed and smiled. "What else?" she asked.

"Her maiden name was Emma Christine Magnusson, before she married Pa. She was about my age when she boarded a steamer in Sweden and crossed the Atlantic." Bernie's eyes turned hazy, as if he could feel the ocean spray in his face. "Wouldn't that be exciting, Al, to take off on such an adventure?"

"What else, Bernie?"

"She worked in a rich family's house in Sweden. Perhaps she thought she'd do the same here, but she settled in Varna with her sister."

"That's our Aunt Tildy," Alice said

"Yep, she stayed with Aunt Tildy until she met a handsome man with a bushy moustache and eyes as dark as the inside of this barn at night." Alice smiled imagining Pa's dark eyes gazing with love at her mother.

Bernie continued. "When Mother and Pa were first married, they set up housekeeping on their own farm. I don't remember much about that place, but I sure remember when little Theolinda was born."

Alice giggled. Bernie liked to tease Minnie by calling her by her unusual middle name. Minnie hated it.

"Yep, our sister Minnie was running the house from the day she was born," he said. "And then you added to the mix a few years later with that howling I've reminded you of. Ma used to sing Swedish tunes in the kitchen as she rocked you to sleep and when she started up the woodstove in the morning. I couldn't wait to get to the table for breakfast. She made the softest rye bread spread with thick slabs of butter from Pa's cows."

"You didn't eat kropkaka for breakfast?" Alice teased. Kropkaka, Swedish potato dumpling with bits of pork, were Bernie's favorite.

Bernie laughed. "Mother made the best breakfast you ever tasted Al! You know better than to make fun of a good bowl of kropkaka!"

A comfortable silence settled over the barn. "Tell me about how she died, Bernie," Alice whispered.

"It was a terrible day, Al. She was expecting a baby. Everyone thought the pregnancy was making her sick, but it was really her appendix. Her appendix burst and she died. I remember neighbors and church folk pouring through the house, bringing food and looking sad. Pa sat in the front room like a stone statue. I don't recall him saying a word to anyone."

"You'd think he'd say *something*," Alice said. "Didn't he talk to you or Minnie? Didn't he cry?"

"Al, I think his heart was broken and no amount of talking or crying would fix it."

All was quiet again, both of them lost in the mournful days. Bernie picked up his rag and Alice stroked the now-sleeping tabby. Neither of them noticed Pa standing in the shadows.

"Reckon it's time to hitch the buggy, Bernie," Pa said. Startled, Al and Bernie jumped up. The cat scrambled for cover.

"Yes, sir," Bernie replied.

Pa limped over to Bernie's bucket-stool and picked it up. He winced a little as he hung it near the cow stall. Alice felt a flash of sympathy for her father. His leg, once broken and never properly set, pained him most of the time. "Is your leg feeling worse, Pa?" she asked.

John Crone turned towards his daughter. In the dim light Alice thought she saw his face soften. "It's fine," he said. "Time to go home, Al."

Pa called her Al - he never did that. The way he said it was almost sweet. Alice sighed. She was sad that "home" did not include Pa.

Pa stepped towards the barn door, pausing with his grip on the handle. "You do look like her, Alice," he said.

"Baby Evelyn?" Alice asked.

"No, your mother" he replied, yanking the door open and limping into the sunshine.

Alice, sitting in the grass.

Chapter 2

Home for Alice was a weathered farmhouse surrounded by endless miles of rich, black dirt. She had lived in this house with just Bernie and Minnie ever since she could remember. Pa had moved to the second farm when he brought home his new wife, using the excuse that it was a good way for Bernie to get his start farming. Alice didn't believe it. She was convinced that her new ma just didn't want to move in with three little kids that weren't her own. That thought made her so sad that she tried not to think of it very often. Minnie said there was no use fussing over something you couldn't change, and she was probably right. Sometimes it was fun, having the farm to themselves with hired hands coming and going, and having visits from Pa all by themselves.

In the early 1900's, corn and oats criss-crossed the land near Wenona, Illinois for as far as a person could see. When Alice and Minnie were little, they played in the fields, winding down the rows of corn, lifting their skirts over the mud clods and imagining themselves trapped in a giant puzzle. They grabbed hands and burst out of the green leaves, happy to find the farmyard exactly where they expected it to be.

No one would get muddy in the field today. It hadn't rained for weeks and the scorching sun had turned the green corn stalks crunchy brown. Day before yesterday, Bernie and Alice had ridden into town for supplies and all the talk was about how poor the harvest would be. Bernie's eyes crinkled with worry. He brightened up, though, when he checked the shopping list and saw that Minnie had asked them to buy more sugar. "There's sure to be a pie cooking if your sister needs more sugar, Al!" Alice laughed until she snorted. Bernie did love pie!

Today Alice could smell peach pie as she trudged across the barnyard. While it was still cool, Minnie was baking pies for the church picnic that afternoon. Alice had worked to be ready too. She had gotten up in the dark, before the heat set in, to do her chores, but sweat was already rolling down her back and beading on her lip. The barn was stifling. The cows fidgeted in their stalls, irritated at Alice's attempts to milk them. "Betsy, settle down!" Alice said. "Just let me finish!" It was a battle. By the time Alice took the foaming white buckets to the house, her eyebrows were crinkled in irritation. She thumped the milk buckets in the corner of the kitchen.

"Alice, it looks like you spilled a little milk on the floor."

"Probably did," Alice snapped, grabbing the tin egg pail and slamming back out the screen door.

"Why, Alice!" Minnie said, her words trailing off as Alice marched back across the barnyard to the chicken coop.

"Honestly," Alice thought to herself. "When I grow up I'm not going to live on a farm!" A rooster ran across her path, nearly tripping her. "Scoot, Jake!" she cried.

A few chicks followed, their mothers who were pecking across the yard. Alice usually enjoyed gathering the eggs from the hen house, but today, in the early heat, she braced herself for the stink. About thirty hens sat protectively on their nests. Feathers and straw flew when she stepped inside, and the agitated hens clucked at her.

"Calm down ladies! You'll break your eggs with all that flapping. Now, let's see if you have any gems this morning." She pushed one hen to the side of her nest and pulled out two warm perfectly shaped eggs. The hen cocked her head to the side, clucking with pride. Alice couldn't help but smile. Alice's belly rumbled. A skillet of scrambled eggs sounded wonderful! Through the winter the hens didn't lay well. It wasn't until Easter that they began to lay mounds of beautiful white eggs. Minnie whipped them up into fluffy meringues and buttery pound cakes. Alice nestled her precious cargo in the pail and hurried to the house. Breakfast was on her mind.

"Got the eggs!" she announced, bursting through the door. Already the kitchen was sweltering. Minnie was pulling three steaming pies from the cook stove oven and placing them on the table to cool. "Yum," Alice said. "I'm starving."

Minnie's hand swept a loose strand of hair back behind her ear. "Breakfast is ready as soon as you wash up."

Alice flopped in a chair, her arms crossed.

"Alice, you've been out of sorts all morning. What is going on?" Minnie asked.

"I guess it's the picnic," Alice said. "I don't want to be stuck helping the ladies, arranging the food and such. I know I'm too old to play the kid games, but anything is more fun than having to listen to the old women talk."

"When I was your age," Minnie said, "I babysat for the little kids. I could play with them if I wanted, I was helping out too. And I didn't have to listen to all the old women talk about boring things."

"That's what I'll do!" Alice exclaimed, her face bright with relief.

"Now let's eat," Minnie said. "We've got a lot to do before we go." Minnie opened the warming oven and took out a platter of golden pancakes with shiny pools of butter on the top. "It'll be just a minute on the eggs, and by then Bernie should be back from tending to the horses." The massive oven smoked as Minnie cracked eggs into the skillet, steam rising from the side compartment where water heated to wash the dishes.

Bernie burst through the door. "I'm starving!" he said. Eyeing the crusty new pies, he opened his mouth to beg for "just a taste," but Minnie pulled him up short with a stern look.

"You'll have to wait for the picnic," Minnie said. "Who knows, maybe you'll find some pretty girl to share a pie with." She and Alice giggled. Bernie's face turned the color of a pickled beet.

"Who's looking for pretty girls?" a deep voice hollered from the porch. In a second, Pa strode through the screen door into the kitchen. Pa's hired man, Gust, followed close behind. Pa was dressed in his Sunday best, a store-bought suit from town. The tailor had measured his arms and legs for a custom fit. He looked handsome, but was already sweating.

"Ma isn't coming today," Pa said, moving to the stove to pour a cup of coffee. "Baby Evelyn isn't doing well in the heat. Phoebe and Orville are outside pestering Nero." As if on cue, the farm dog yapped with excitement. "So Bernie, I do suppose there will be some young ladies at the picnic today," Pa smiled.

"Well, uh, as to the pretty girls, I'm not really looking, you see, Bernie stammered. It's just the pie that interests me."

Everyone burst out laughing. Minnie whisked a steaming plate of eggs onto the table just as Phoebe and Orville burst in.

"Phoebe, can I be your babysitter at the picnic?" Alice asked.

"Sure!" Phoebe said, clapping her hands with delight. In minutes, the family gathered around the table. They dug into the stack of pancakes, pile of eggs and crisp bacon. Alice savored the first fluffy bite of pancake, dripping with warm syrup, and thought this was the best breakfast she'd had in a long time.

Martin, "Frosty."

Chapter

3

The timber was magical. Just a few miles west of town, it was a tangle of trees and bushes, stumps and rocks. Hollowed-out logs and overgrown brush hid hundreds of animals. Years ago, Osage Indians hunted deer and snared rabbits in this same forest. They fished the deep water of Sandy Creek that now beckoned hot feet to cool off and feel fish slip against their ankles. The timber's cool green shade and soothing water had been a blessed relief to many on a boiling summer day.

Though Pa had brought the biggest buggy, the ride to the timber was dusty and crowded. Gust and Minnie held Orville and Phoebe on their laps. Five year old Phoebe, wiggled her red and white gingham dress a wrinkled mess by the time they arrived. Seven year old Orville, sulked at the insult of sitting on someone's lap. Alice was squished against Bernie. Her dark pigtails slapped him in the head as the buggy jostled along the bumpy road. Dust and pebbles peppered their faces. By the time they pulled into the meadow, everyone in the buggy was cross.

"Phoebe, you're stepping on my dress!" Minnie scold-ed as they piled out. "Orville, don't tip that pie!"

"Gust, can you unhitch the team?" Pa asked irritably. "Bernie, help Minnie with the food."

"Yes sir," Bernie grumbled.   Young men were gathered at the far end of the meadow, unpacking a croquet set. Bernie eyed the cluster of women setting up the food. "I'm off with the pies, Min," he said, and strode away.

"Gust do you need help with the horses?" Al asked, reaching for Beauty's neck, slick with sweat.

Gust and Pa were talking in hushed tones and pointing down the hill, where a group of people moved between cooking fires and tattered tents.   Alice could see dark-skinned children playing with hoops and sticks, and mustached men smoking and laughing. "Who are they, Pa?" Alice asked.

"Never you mind, Alice," Pa said abruptly. "Go on to the picnic."

"But I said I'd help Gust with the horses."

"No need Alice," Gust said. "I'll tend to the pair."

Alice picked a handful of grass and held it up to Anna, Beauty's lively daughter.   Anna's coat had been fuzzy and light when she was a colt, but now it was brownish black like Beauty's. A whinny from one of the other teams caught Anna's attention and she nickered a reply. "You'll have lots of horse friends to visit while we're gone," Alice laughed, the strangers forgotten. "Phoebe, are you ready to find the other kids? My guess is they're down by the creek!" Phoebe squealed and clapped her hands and Alice laughed. "We're going to find Frosty, Pa," Alice said. "I'll take good care of Phoebe." Alice called back as they took off at a run.

It was easy to find Frosty in a crowd of people. His white blonde hair had earned him his nickname when he was a baby. Al and Frosty were born a year apart, and had been friends as long as she could remember.

"Keep up, Phoeb! I think I hear everyone!" The narrow path to the creek was overgrown with bushes and sheltered by oaks and pines. Al didn't stop to marvel at the massive trees that crowded their way, but Phoebe did. Her curious eyes followed the huge trunks, their hundreds of branches shooting into the sun. Magical.

"Oh Al!" Phoebe cried suddenly, clapping with excitement. "Strawberries!" Alice looked back and followed Phoebe's finger pointing to a patch of wild strawberry bushes off the path.

Alice's mouth watered. There was nothing like the sweet taste of wild strawberries.

"Oh alright, we'll stop but let's pick 'em quick." Cupping the front of their skirts, the girls loaded their laps with plump red berries. They ate as fast as they picked, it wasn't long before they were headed down the path again, cradling the berries. They burst onto the creek bottom.

"We've got berries!" Phoebe yelled to the children playing on the bank. With a whoop they gathered around the girls, giggling and grabbing.

"Hi Al!" Frosty greeted her. "Where'd you find these?"

"Just off the path." Alice said. A group of kids were back down at the water's edge, busily poking under rocks and splashing in the muddy water.

"What's everyone looking for?" Alice asked.

"Leeches, minnows and craw daddies. Elmer and George brought fishing poles and they've had a couple of bites." Frosty picked up two slimy dead fish. "See? There's some big ones just waiting to be hooked."

From deep in the woods they heard a loud whistle. "Dinnertime!" Frosty cried. They clamored to pick up shoes and race up the hill.

The makeshift tables groaned under the heaping plates of food. Alice fidgeted through the long prayer, eager to eat. The food served at the Bethany Lutheran Church picnic was truly a feast. The women had picked the best recipes and competed to serve the most delicious dishes. The men had butchered a hog that appeared on the table as baked ham, trimmed with sweet potatoes and brown sugar. Chickens from the henhouse were fried golden brown. The bin in each family's cellar had kept the potatoes cool until they were mashed with butter and cream. Fresh garden tomatoes, squash and beans were mixed into tangy salads, and berries and apples baked into flaky pies. There were angel food cakes, fresh sugar cookies and irresistible homemade ice cream. The men and boys spent hours cranking the handles of the wooden ice cream freezers. Alice's favorite was the fresh peach ice cream. She closed her eyes and let spoonful after spoonful of the cool sweetness slide down down her throat.

"Alice, where's Phoebe?" Pa demanded, suddenly right at her elbow. His face was red and worried.

Alice's heart thumped. Where *had* she last seen Phoeb? She had been so busy eating that she had forgotten about watching Phoebe.

"I don't know, Pa," she stammered. "We came up from the creek together. I got her a piece of watermelon a little bit ago, and she and Orville were spitting seeds at a chipmunk over by that log."

"Orville has been playing stick ball with the boys for over an hour and no one has seen Phoebe." Pa's face twitched. He didn't say it, but Alice knew he wanted to add, "Weren't you supposed to be babysitting her, Alice?" She felt sick to her stomach. "We need to spread out and search. Pa continued. Alice, head back by the buggies to see if she went to visit the horses."

"I'll help too, Mr. Crone," Frosty offered.

Pa nodded and turned to Gust and Mr. Johnson who were walking towards them. "Any luck?" he asked. They shook their heads. Gust pulled Pa aside. Alice heard him murmur "Gypsies" before Frosty tugged at her arm.

"Let's run, Al. Sounds like Phoebe is good and lost."

Alice's chest pounded. Gypsies! That was who was camping in the bottom of the field. Alice had heard about their dark skin and strange foreign ways. They didn't have permanent homes, but traveled in groups through the countryside, gleaning leftover crops from the fields and selling trinkets in towns along the way. She'd overheard the grownups say they stole things from honest people. It seemed grownups were a little scared of the Gypsies.

Beauty whinnied a greeting as Alice and Frosty ran up, nearly out of breath. "No sign of her here, Al," Frosty said. He searched in the buggy and checked underneath.

"Where could she have gone, Frosty? I just couldn't bear it if something happened to her!"

"Don't talk like that, Alice. I'm sure she's around here somewhere. I'm going to check the water hole. You stay here in case she shows up."

Alice stroked Anna's mane thinking of Phoebe's bubbly laugh and bright eyes. She should have taken better care of her little sister! This wasn't the first time she had been careless with Phoebe. When Phoebe had been a baby and Alice had only been eight years old, cousin Perle came for a visit, and Alice and Perle sat on the front steps of the house, taking turns holding Phoebe. Phoebe started to squirm, so the girls moved to a couch on the farmhouse porch. When they sat down hundreds of bees swarmed from a hole in the sofa cushions. They filled Alice's eyes and ears with insane terrifying buzzes and sharp stings. She and Perle ran screaming into the yard, flailing their hands and arms to get away from the bees. In their panic, they left Phoebe on the couch – the very couch that contained the raging bees! Within seconds the screaming baby was covered with bees. Her tiny face, hands, arms and legs swelled with red, angry welts. Alice shuddered. Phoebe had almost died from her neglect, now it was happening all over again! Alice started to cry.

"Al!" Frosty said, returning from the water hole. "It won't do any good to cry. Think. Is there *any* place Phoebe might have gone? Retrace your steps in your mind. Where did you go when you left the buggy? Any special spot she might have gone back to?"

"Yes! The strawberry patch! Maybe she went back to the strawberry patch!"

"Let's go. You lead the way."

It wasn't hard to find the strawberry patch again. They didn't see Phoebe, but Alice recognized the bushes where she and Phoebe had picked the first berries. And now the bushes further back had also been picked clean. In fact, Alice noticed, there didn't seem to be any strawberries left at all.

Loud hollers rang through the forest, calling Phoebe's name. They echoed sadly as no one replied. "Maybe we should head back," Frosty said. "Someone might have found her by now."

"Wait, there's something funny about this patch." Alice said as she walked further out into the berry bushes. She scanned the timber and looked into the distant fields. Her eyes locked on a group of people in the clearing below and her heart jumped. "Frosty, look. It's the gypsies." The gypsies were moving out of the meadow in a line, their brightly colored caravan exotic and out of place

amidst the dull, dry corn. A tambourine ching-chinged
the rhythm and a deep voice sang. At the end of the line a
slim woman with long, untied hair held the hand of a little
girl with a red and white gingham dress. Phoebe!

Frosty was the first to move. Gulping, he said, "Let's
run back to the picnic and tell your Pa."

"By then it will be too late," Alice replied. "The gypsies might be gone, and they'll take Phoebe with them!"

"What else can we do?" Frosty asked.

"I'm going down to get her," Alice said.

Frosty's mouth hung open in surprise. Alice almost
lost her nerve. "Frosty, you go back and get my Pa. I'll go
after Phoebe and if I run into trouble, you and Pa will be
close behind. Now run!"

Listening to Frosty's retreating footsteps, Alice shivered. "It's up to you," she told herself. "This time you
need to save Phoebe." She took a deep breath and ran to
catch up with the gypies.

As Alice neared the end of the ragged line, she could
make out Phoebe's voice. She was laughing and singing with the dark young woman. Bright new ribbons
bounced in her curls. "Phoebe!" Alice yelled. No one
turned around. Alice ran faster. Panting, she called out
once again. "Phoebe!"

Phoebe and the woman turned at the same time, still
hand in hand. Alice caught a delighted look of surprise as
Phoebe's face lit up upon seeing her, but the young woman glared at her. Phoebe waved with both hands, raced
to Alice, and garnered the attention of the entire caravan.
"Al, look at my tambourine and my pretty ribbons!" she
cried.

Alice hugged her sister with relief, tears welling up
in her brown eyes. "Beautiful, Phoeb. But you shouldn't

have run off. Everyone was so worried."

Phoebe looked puzzled. "I didn't run off. Mardelana helped me pick more strawberries, then asked me to come play with her for awhile."

By that time the group of gypsies had encircled the sisters. Alice looked into each unfamiliar face and shivered again under their gazes. Mardelana sneered as their eyes met. She tossed her head, the gold charms on her ears jingling.

"Mardelana, is this true?" A deep boomed voice from the crowd.   A dark, handsome man stepped to the circle. With folded arms he stood in front of the young woman and waited for her to answer.

"Yes," Mardelana replied defiantly.   "I asked her to play. I thought it would be fun to have someone new in our group. There were certainly extra children in the timber. I didn't think she'd be missed."

The dark man gave her a hard look and said, "We will talk later." He laid a hand softly on Alice's shoulder and said, "I am sorry to have troubled you, Miss. My daughter means well, but is headstrong. Perhaps you are headstrong yourself sometimes." Alice blushed. Yes, she knew about being headstrong. The dark man turned to Phoebe. "Thank you, little sunshine, for bringing your light to our group for awhile. Now hurry back with your sister."

Turning to Alice again, the man said, "Please tell your father that we meant no harm, and no harm has come to your little Miss Sunshine." He touched Phoebe's head lightly, his fingers pausing on her bright ribbons. Then he turned to take his place at the front of the caravan. The tambourine and the singing started once again and the gypsies moved forward.

"Phoebe," Alice said, "Pa is terribly worried. Hold my

hand we need to hurry back. Let's run!" It wasn't long before they rounded the hill and saw Pa, Frosty and a group of men headed towards them. The girls shouted a greeting and the men waved back. Even from the distance, Pa looked relieved. Alice knelt down in front of Phoebe and hugged her tight. "Phoebe," she said. "Let's keep your pretty ribbons in my dress pocket until we get home. OK? We'll put them in a safe place and they'll be our little secret." But Alice believed there was magic, or at least good luck, in those gypsy ribbons. Alice knew Pa would never approve them keeping anything that belonged to these gypsies.

Phoebe's eyes sparkled. "OK," she whispered. "I love secrets."

The picnic ended at sunset with singing by the campfire. Phoebe burrowed her head into Alice's lap, her eyelids fluttering closed.

"Alice." She stiffened at Pa's voice behind her. He had spoken very little since their return from the gypsies.

"Yes, Pa?"

"About Phoebe getting lost," he began.

"I'm so sorry Pa," Alice whispered fearfully. "I was supposed to be watching her the whole time, and I let her get away from me, and who knows what might have happened..."

"Alice, I just wanted to say that I was very proud of the way you went after Phoebe by yourself. You were very brave." In the smoky dusk, Pa squeezed her shoulder and moved into the shadows. Alice smiled. She *had* saved Phoebe this time. She looked down at her sleeping sister and imagined that Phoebe was dreaming of dancing gypsies, bright ribbons and jingling tambourines.

Chapter 4

Later that summer, Alice yelled across the churchyard as she arrived for the last day of Swedish School. "Frosty, Pa said I could come home with you after class!" Frosty ran over, flashing a grin. "Great! Paul even let me bring the buggy so we could ride home in style."

"You brought the team to school all by yourself? Do you think you can get us back home in once piece?"

"I won't be all by myself," Frosty said confidently. "You'll be with me if I run into any trouble." Alice crinkled her eyebrows into a worried look and Frosty just laughed.

It took a strong yank to open the double doors of the church. Alice and Frosty were the first ones to arrive and the church was cool and serene. Since it was the last day, Frosty's mother had made him wear a button-up wool jacket and necktie with his knickers and thick socks. He pulled on his collar and muttered that it was good to be out of the sun. Alice smoothed her dress and soaked up the quiet. She loved the church when it was empty. It felt like it belonged just to her. They had just a minute to settle on one of the hard pews before Perle and George, two of Alice's cousins, burst through the door.

"Quit George!" Perle said. "I said I didn't want to race."

"Only 'cause you knew I'd win," George teased.

"Honestly," Perle replied, flipping her blonde pigtails. "Wait 'til Ma hears you were in running in church!"

Before too long the rest of the kids arrived. About forty children attended Swedish School in the summer months. There were six-year-olds all the way up to teenagers gathering every weekday from morning until early afternoon. From the minute they walked in, they spoke only Swedish. It was exhausting to translate every thought into Swedish before speaking. Frosty often spit out his sentences with half the words in Swedish and half in English. The class would burst out laughing and Mr. Swenson, their teacher, would turn red and rap his ruler on the desk. Mr. Swenson didn't approve of laughter.

Each summer their instructor was a different seminary student from Augustana College. Mr. Swenson was a very somber man with no hair and big ears. Oversized glasses made his eyes look tiny. He squinted them at the first sign of noise. When he was really angry, he gulped giant mouthfuls of air, making his skinny bowtie bob up and down on his Adam's apple. Mr. Swenson stayed at Mrs. Nelson's house, as all the visiting students did. Alice thought it was a good thing old Mrs. Nelson didn't make much noise.

The class recited passages in Swedish and read from a Swedish bible. It was the hymns, however, that captured Alice's heart. The melodies rolled off her lips and burst out in sweet sounds. Alice liked to imagine her real mother, Emma, singing those same hymns in the church in Kristdala, Sweden. "It's like Mother is singing with me," Alice thought.

At noon the children spread out in the shade of a tow-

ering oak tree next to the church. Pulling out their lunch
baskets, they munched freshly baked bread and hunks of
salty sausage. Most had fresh milk in a quart jar and a
few shared cookies or a piece of Angel Food cake. Alice
grinned as she opened her basket. Minnie had packed
fresh pancakes, rolled and stuffed with sugar and blue-
berries, just like Alice liked them.

"So Alice," Perle asked. "I heard you're going out to
Frosty's place for supper? Your Pa let you?"

"Yep," Alice replied happily. "I just up and asked him,
since it was the last day of Swede School and I wouldn't
see Frosty much except Sundays. I couldn't believe it! He
just said, 'Alice, my little flicka, you just go right ahead.'"

Alice crossed her fingers behind her back, sorry to be
telling such a lie. The truth was, Pa didn't think much
of her going to Frosty's. She'd begged and pleaded and
finally Pa had given in. Surprisingly, Ma had been over
to the farm and had urged her support. "Let her go, John,
the Appletons are good folk, and Alice has been such a
help with the young ones this summer. She deserves some
time off." Except for Swede School, and church on Sundays, Alice, Bernie and Minnie had plenty of work to be
done on the farm. There was little time for socializing.
Visiting for dinner was a special treat. Alice was so happy
she hugged Pa, then Ma. Ma stiffened at her touch, but
Alice imagined that Ma hugged her back.

The afternoon passed quickly and soon the students
were saying goodbye and tossing their baskets in the
buggy. "Whoa, girls," Frosty murmured to his team as he
hitched them for the ride to the farm. Al helped by stroking Darling's thick mane.

Alice loved visiting the Appleton farm. The square
farmhouse was homey and busy. Frosty had three older

brothers, an older sister, and a younger sister, Clara, who reminded Alice of Phoebe. The Appleton farm was just down the road from the Lindgrens and the Kuehns, where there were even more kids to play with. "I can't wait to get there," she said to Frosty. "I just love all the commotion at your house!"

The drive from town was breezy. Frosty handled the feisty horses like an expert, being careful not to let them go too fast and get overheated. As they approached the house, Alice could see Mrs. Appleton on the east side, taking washing off the long clothesline. When she heard the approaching buggy, she turned and waved. Mrs. Appleton had a broad smile and a slight figure. She wore a faded bonnet, which protected the delicate, fair skin Alice had always admired. The tough life of the farm took its toll on her good looks. Gentle wrinkles on her face reflected the work of raising six children and the pain of losing two. Little Nils had died when he was one year old, and baby Sisel when she was one month old. Alice remembered their tiny gravestones in the Swedish cemetery.

"Hello, you two!" cried a familiar voice. Alice hadn't even noticed Frosty's older sister, Minnie, on the east porch by the ironing board. As they pulled into the barnyard, Alice could see that Minnie was finishing a pile of starching and ironing. At least there was a cool whiff of wind to take the edge off this sweltering work. Minnie had heated the bottom of the iron on the cookstove and carried it to the porch. They had two metal plate bottoms, so one could be heating while the iron itself was snapped onto the other bottom to keep the job going. Alice had seen her own sister Minnie iron for hours. It was a blistering job, especially in the summer when the cookstove blazed. Pa didn't like Alice to iron, since she had burned one of his best shirts by leaving the fiery iron on one spot for too long.

"Hi Minnie," Alice replied, nimbly from the buggy. "Hello, Mrs. Appleton," she said, to Frosty's mother as she rounded the corner, wiping her hands on her apron.

"Hello, Alice," Mrs. Appleton said warmly. Minnie and I were just taking a break for a cup of coffee. Why don't you join us? Martin, after you take care of the horses, come on in. I have a special treat for you and your guest."

Frosty grimaced at the mention of his given name. "Yes ma'am," he replied and headed off with the team. "Hey, Snap," Frosty called to a dusty dog sniffing around the barnyard. Snap skidded to a stop at the sound of Frosty's voice. Panting, he raced over and jumped up on Frosty nearly knocking him over. "Hey boy," Frosty laughed. "Not so wild!"

Inside the house, Alice smelled something wonderful cooking. "Raspberries pies?" Alice asked. "You guessed," Mrs. Appleton smiled as she pulled off her bonnet. "Would you like a few berries?" Alice nodded.

Mrs. Appleton reached for two bowls. "Martin's favorite," she said. Heaping bright berries into the bowls and pouring thick cream on top. From the heavy metal coffeepot, she poured streams of coffee into dainty flowered cups. Settling between Minnie and Alice, she smoothed her gray-tinged bun and gracefully sipped her coffee as Frosty burst through the door.

"Berries!" he said, quickly washing his hands. He sniffed the air. "And raspberry pie for dessert?" he asked incredulously.

"Yes, Martin," Mrs. Appleton replied with a smile. "In honor of Alice's visit. Do you think you can eat raspberries twice in one day," she asked.

"You know I can," Martin said with a grin.

After their treat, Alice and Martin met some of the neighbor kids who walked over from the Lindgren farms. Chores completed for the day, Paul was organizing a game of baseball. They used a heavy stick for a bat and a well-worn ball, made from strips of rag rolled round and round. Alice raced to help lay out the bases. It was a pretty fair game, with only one time-out as they searched for the ball Fred hit into the cornfield. The only injury was a skinned knee as Clarence slid into second.

Dinner was delicious. Mr. Appleton and older brothers Ansfred and Art joined them from the fields, and Mr. Appleton led the crowded table in grace. Mrs. Appleton served Alice's favorites – fried chicken cooked in a heavy black skillet, milky mashed potatoes and thick, peppered gravy. Alice couldn't help smothering the warm biscuits and fresh sweet corn with big gobs of butter. "Clarence's mother sent over the butter," Mrs. Appleton said. "She churns fifteen pounds of butter a week and brings it to Beckman's store to sell. People from all over the county ask for Mrs. Lindgren's butter."

Alice barely had room for the delicious raspberry pie. After they'd finished, Mr. Appleton smoothed his straw-colored moustache. "Excellent meal, Emma," he nodded. Turning to Frosty, he added, "Are you planning to take Alice home in the buggy, or would you like me to?"

Frosty puffed up with pride. "I will, Pa."

"Do you think you need a hand?"

"No, Pa. I've been back and forth from Swede School with no problem."

"Alright then, you best get going so you can get back while it's still light. You two may be excused from the table."

Thanking Mr. and Mrs. Appleton, Alice cleared her

spot at the table and followed Frosty to the barn. It wasn't long before they had the team harnessed, and were leading them to the road. Snap swerved in and out, barking goodbye. "Shoo, Snap," Frosty said. "Get back to the house, boy."

"Frosty, I had such a great time," Alice said. "You have such a nice, normal family."

"Only because everyone was on their best behavior," Frosty teased. "Usually we're anything but normal."

The team was tired and eased out of the farmyard at a sluggish walk. Frosty held the reins loosely and pointed to the early evening lightning bugs. "Look at them glittering by the rosebushes, Al."

All of a sudden, with an ear-splitting squawk, a flurry of feathers exploded under the horses' hindquarters. They bucked violently as Snap came shooting out of the grassy ditch, barking and yapping at a pair of pheasants. "Hang on, Al!" Frosty yelled, as the horses jerked desperately to the right and plunged into the dry corn. The stalks slapped at Alice's face and cut into her hands as she gripped the side of the buggy.

"Frosty!" she screamed. "Stop them!"

"Whoa!" Frosty yelled, pulling back on the reins as hard as he could. "Whoa girls!" The horses plunged ahead, ears laid back. Frosty's frantic pulling on the reins didn't slow them a bit. The team circled round in the field and raced back over the road, angling for a minute towards the farmhouse where Mrs. Appleton was screaming something she couldn't understand from the east porch. The men seemed to be running, though Alice couldn't see where the horses galloped back into the corn. Alice ducked her head again as the stalks tore at her hair.

"Al, we better jump!" Frosty yelled. The thundering of

horse hoofs and the crashing of the corn was deafening.

"Jump?" Alice asked with disbelief. "We'll be killed!"

"The wagon's going to tip!" Frosty yelled back. "I'll count to three then bail off the side! On three. One, two, three, go!" Alice gripped the rough sides of the jostling wagon terrified to jump. "Al, go!" Frosty screamed.

Alice dove to the right and felt stiff corn leaves slice into her arms and legs. With a groan she thudded onto the dry earth. The horses crashed on by, and after a moment, it was quiet.

"Frosty!" Alice stammered, looking around her. "Are you alright?" She heard a reply not too far away.

"I'm here. I think I'm OK."

Gingerly Alice stretched her arms and legs, amazed she could still move. Frosty was soon by her side, helping her up. She was shocked to see him grinning.

"Just what are you smiling about?" she snapped, shocked. "We could have been killed!"

"Yes, but we weren't," he said. "It sure feels great to be standing on the ground."

"Martin! Alice!" people called out. Mr. Appleton, on horseback, met them just as they were staggering back through the wide swath of trampled corn. "Thank goodness you're alright!" he said, dismounting quickly and hugging the two.

"Pa, I'm so sorry about the wagon," Frosty said, now remembering the damage done.

"I'm just glad you two are safe."

"Have you seen the horses?" Frosty asked.

"Yep, they circled back to the house and are just fine – except for being plum tuckered out."

"Like me," Al murmured weakly.

Frosty and Mr. Appleton laughed. "We'll get you

back to the house and Emma will fix you right up, Alice," said Mr. Appleton comfortingly. "You'll be feeling better soon."

"Anyway, Al," Frosty added. "That little adventure wasn't anything an extra slice of raspberry pie couldn't fix!" At that, Alice smiled at last.

Alice and friends, on footbridge.

Chapter 5

Fall turned to an early winter, and the schoolhouse stove gobbled wood by the armload. The boys took turns feeding logs through the black metal doors. Today was Frosty's turn. And today, Frosty's bright yellow hair was on fire.

Clara was the first to notice. "Frosty's on fire!" she screamed. Frosty didn't realize she was yelling about him until he felt the flames. Before he could let out a holler, a hand grabbed the back of his neck and plunged his head into the water bucket. Frosty jerked his head back out and water flew over the wooden floor.

His schoolmates stood staring, their mouths wide open. His bulging blue eyes stared back. "Am I still alive?" he asked, water dripping from his nose. Everyone laughed, relieved to see Frosty joking and safe. Fred Kuehn was the first to clap him on the back.

When Mrs. Hine asked you to stoke the fire in the wood-stove, I don't think she meant for you to use your head!"

"Oh Frosty," Clara said, wide eyed. "The ends of your hair is burnt off!" The fire had singed the tips of Frosty's locks, leaving his hair blackened and wet.

"Okay, who dunked my head," Frosty teased.

"I did, young man," responded Mrs. Hine, fanning her pale face from her seat near the stove. "Mrs. Hine," said Clara, "you saved Frosty's life. His head was smoking!"

The room filled with laughter. Then Mrs. Hine gathered herself up and announced, "That will be the end of school today." The class cheered. "I'll put the fire out myself," she added with a smile.

The six students in the Trimont School hurried to flip up the tops of their desks and push their books, slates and pencils inside.

Frosty and Clara gathered up their lunch baskets and carefully packed the wide-mouth soup jars of sausage and potatoes to heat for lunch on the pot-bellied stove. They topped their warm lunch with bread and jelly. Today Frosty packed it tightly for the bumpy ride home. He and Clara had ridden horseback to school. "Best bundle up, Clara, it's going to be a cold ride home."

"I wish we could have hitched a ride in Clarence's buggy," Clara grumbled.

"Aw Clara, quit your complaining. Clarence didn't even bring the buggy today. That's only for muddy days."

"Well then, I wish it was muddy," Clara pouted.

"If it was muddy," Frosty teased, "it would probably be spring, which would mean Christmas would have passed you right by."

Clara's eyes popped open wide. "No, I didn't mean I wanted to miss Christmas!"

"I didn't think so, little lady. Now up you go," Frosty chuckled as he boosted Clara onto the horse. It was an easier journey on the nicer days when they rode their bikes the quarter mile to the school.

Trimont School was named after a ship that had brought Irish immigrants to America. Students at Trimont always wondered what happened to those Irish immigrants, since most of the people they knew came from Sweden. Frosty's father, Nils August Hakenson, had emigrated from the town of Appelkulla, Sweden, when he was twenty. He, his brother and sister had come to America and taken the name Appleton after his little village. Frosty's Ma had been sixteen when she journeyed across the ocean to America. She was on the steamer for weeks, sick from the rolling ocean waves, hoping each day to see land.

"Frosty, hurry him along!" Clara urged. "I'm freezing!"

They rounded the corner from the Kuehn farm and could see their own white house up the road. The cozy kitchen light glowed on the chilly December day.

"Frosty, what are all those buggies doing at the farm?" Clara asked, curious.

"I don't know. What a crowd."

"Oh, it's the Cheesing! I forgot all about it! Good thing we're home early so we can help!"

Frosty groaned. Every December the women got together to make traditional Swedish cheeses. The house would be bustling with gossip and chatter. As they pulled into the barnyard, there was no sign of Pa or the older boys. They had escaped.

"Help me down, Frosty," Clara begged as they came to a stop. Clara rushed in the house to join the action. Frosty walked the horse to the barn, wondering how long he could hide out, putting up the horse and tending to its stall. Soon, his stomach drove him inside for his after-school snack of rye bread and sausage. Thinking about his blackened hair he decided to leave his hat on.

Ma was in the middle of the story when he walked in. He sliced off a hunk of warm bread, spread it thick with butter and crept off to a corner to listen. "Our people back in Sweden had the tradition of gathering together for a cheese-making party before Christmas. Sometimes we have the party at the parsonage, the preacher's house."

"Who brought all the milk?" Clara blurted, eyeing the many cans lined up against the wall.

"Everyone brought a can of fresh milk," Ma said. "Then we poured them into the wash boilers and heated them on the stove."

"And all you got from all that milk was those few round cheeses?" Clara asked wide-eyed.

All the ladies laughed, their coffee cups tittering on their saucers. "Yes, Clara," Ma said. "It takes ten gallons of milk to make one five-pound cheese. We add rennet to the milk and stir with our big ladles until the curds begin to form. Then we let it set and the curds separate. Next we dip out the curds and scoop them into steamers."

"Are we ready to press the curds yet?" Clara asked.

"We have to put in the cheesecloth lining first, then we'll let you try," Ma replied.

"Press slowly," Mrs. Lindgren added, "or it'll squirt through the cloth and all over your ma's clean floor."

"Martin, can you do me a favor?" Ma asked.

Frosty squirmed, not too excited to leave his corner. "Sure, Ma."

"We need to salt these pressed cheeses into the round molds and set them in a warm, dry place. I think your corner is the warmest."

Clara laughed. "You got bumped out of your spot!"

"I've survived worse, today," he said, winking.

Clara's eyes grew wide as she remembered Frosty's singed hair. "Oh Ma, have I got a story for you!" Frosty rolled his eyes and made a quick run for the barn.

DISTRICT N°7 WENONA ILL. APRIL, 10, 1908. MISS HINES, TEACHER.

April 10, 1908 Frosty standing beside Miss Hines.

Swedish Cheesing (Ostkalas), 1906.

<u>Back Row</u> *(left to right): Mrs. Alfred Helander, Mrs. Gust Claussen, Mrs. August Lindgren, Mrs. (Rev.) Gustaf Erickson (holding cheese), Mrs. August Appleton, Mrs. August Bergsten, Mrs. John Swanson, Mrs. Oscar Johnson.*
<u>Middle Row</u>*: Mrs. Ed Nelson, Mrs. Oscar Hylin, Mrs. Algot Flesberg, Mrs. John Holmstrom, Sr., Mrs. C.O. Flesberg, Mrs. Charles Esterdahl, Mrs. Anna Engstrand (holding son Jerome).* <u>Children</u>*: Elof hylin (on step above), Leonard Flesberg, Inez and Iner Helander, Mildred and Everett Flesberg.*

Chapter

6

Alice couldn't remember such a cold winter. "Min, I've never heard the wind howl like this," she chattered as she pulled the blanket closer. Minnie nudged her sister a little nearer to the stove and opened the iron door to shovel in a scoop of coal.

"The wind sounds terrible, doesn't it?" Minnie replied. She clanged the door shut and flattened her hands to warm her palms. "I wish Bernie would come in out of the snow. I'm afraid he'll get lost out in this mess."

"He'll be alright. I watched him tie off to the porch. Bernie had seen the blizzard coming and he gathered all the horses and cows into the barn before the storm blew out his lantern and made everything white. Alice knew after he fed and watered the animals, he would use the rope to guide him through the whiteout to the front porch. No doubt he was fussing over the younger animals, knowing that they might freeze in the drafty barn.

"Al, move a little closer to me," Minnie suggested. "I just can't seem to get warm. I'm sick and tired of this blizzard."

Alice snuggled closer, surprised to hear Minnie complain. In truth, this was the second day of the fierce storm and it was jangling all of their nerves. "Thank goodness we have enough coal," Alice thought. She hated to think what they would have done without a good supply. Lucky for them, Bernie had brought in a load from town just last week. Wenona was famous for coal, and it was a sure bet that the town wouldn't run out. The Wenona Coal Company, opened in 1873, mined the best soft coal in the area. Nearly 450 men and boys worked at the mine, bringing up 1000 tons of coal a day.

Minnie's harsh cough caught Alice's attention. "Maybe we should go up to bed, Min? It's so late." On these cold nights, they rotated in front of the stove and warmed up every side of their bodies before dashing for the freezing bedroom. Right now, leaving the fire didn't sound very appealing.

"No, we need to wait on Bernie. I have some coffee on the stove and he'll probably want a cup."

The door burst open with a flurry of icy wind and a white blast of snow. A dark figure emerged from the cloud. Al recognized Bernie's red wool cap under a mound of white. "Bernie, your moustache has icicles!" Al exclaimed. Bernie stepped forward, leaving the door wide open.

"Close that door…" Minnie scolded, and then stopped suddenly when she saw what was trailing behind her brother. Minnie and Alice could not believe their eyes. Behind Bernie, clomping snow onto the floor, was Bernie's favorite horse, Pal.

Bernie closed the blowing door, then sheepishly faced his astonished sisters. Pulling his hat from his head, he stammered. "I couldn't just let him freeze in the barn."

Al threw back her head and laughed. In her whole life she never thought she'd see Pal standing in their kitchen, looking like he was ready to sit right down to dinner. She laughed so hard her face turned red and her stomach hurt. Bernie, his moustache dripping icicles, added to the funny picture. It took a couple of moments for Al to realize that Minnie was not laughing.

"Bernie Crone, what are you thinking? Get that smelly old horse out of the kitchen!"

"Aw, Min, you know he's been a little on the frail side after taking sick last fall. He'll freeze to death in the barn."

"I suppose, you'll be asking me to cook up some buck-wheat pancakes in the morning for Pal too?" Minnie asked, tapping her foot. Minnie didn't seem too cold now, Alice noted. "And you'll happily shovel out my kitchen in the morning? I can imagine the breakfast smells right now. Sizzling bacon mixed with fresh horse droppings."

"Come on, Min. It's just for one night, and I'll have him out early. I've been struggling for hours to board up the barn against this wind and it's almost midnight. I'm sure the worst will be over by sunrise, so that's just a little more time for Pal to stay inside."

Al could see Minnie was losing the argument. She was tempted to giggle, but thought better of it when she heard Minnie stifle another cough. Wearily, Minnie conceded. "Pal can stay but he has to be out by sunrise and you'll clean up every last mess until this kitchen smells like roses."

"Yes ma'am," Bernie replied, winking at Alice. "Let's all get some sleep," he said, wiping the last of the snow from Pal's back.

It was a short night. Al opened her eyes to a hint of light in the east, but didn't want to move from underneath the warm quilts. The wind had stopped howling. Seconds later, the front door slammed.

"BERNIE!" bellowed a voice from below. Pa! Alice's

heart pounded. Pa was here? So early? Why did he sound so angry? Minnie sat up in bed. They looked at each other and both remembered at the same time - Pal!

Alice flew down the stairs with Minnie close at her heels. They didn't notice how cold their feet were against the freezing floor. Rounding the corner into the kitchen Al skidded to a stop. Minnie kept going and knocked them both right into Pa. Bernie was hopping on one foot, struggling to pull on his boot as he tried to avoid piles of horse manure.

Pa was fuming. Alice thought she could actually see smoke coming out of his ears. His moustache trembled on his lip like a wiggling caterpillar and his hard-set jaw worked back and forth as if he was chewing foul-tasting leather. Alice and Minnie stood paralyzed. Pa clenched his fists and then angrily stuffed them in his pockets. Opening his mouth in a thin, black line, he glared at Bernie and hissed, "Get that horse out."

Later that day, Al had to admit that she hadn't been this warm in days. The three of them had spent two hours scooping and sweeping the floor. They'd split up the scouring, with Bernie and Alice hand scrubbing the boards while Minnie worked on the table. Pal had drooled all over the top and also raided the sugar bowl. Lucky for them, Pa had been checking on the animals in the barn for most of the time, so they hadn't had to work under his cold stare. Minnie wheezed and coughed as she worked. "Really, I'm sorry," Bernie had started, but Alice and Minnie waved him off.

"It's alright, Bernie." Al assured him. "We did the right thing for Pal."

By afternoon the kitchen sparkled but Minnie was back in bed. "Try some hot milk and honey," Alice urged.

Minnie replied with a congested rumble. "I'm going to put together a wrap for your chest, Min. That'll fix you right up." Alice carefully pulled a woolen cloth from the medicine cabinet. Al knew that a mixture of goose grease and turpentine would make a strong paste. She bypassed the castor oil with a wrinkle of her nose. Fish oil was the worst thing she'd ever smelled but it was good for digestive problems. Goose grease and turpentine didn't smell very good either, so Al worked quickly to rub it on Minnie's chest and cover it with a cloth. "You'll feel better soon," Alice assured her, backing out of the room quietly.

"Alice." Pa startled her as she padded down the hallway. "I have more chores for you in the kitchen."

"Yes, Pa" Alice replied glumly. It seemed it would take a lot of work to pay for Pal's night inside.

Alice folded a basket of clothes that she and Minnie had laundered. They had hung outside as the chilly air swept in and had frozen stiff. The one-piece union suit underwear sat propped up like icy scarecrows as they thawed in front of the stove. Pa and Bernie milked the cows, and Bernie and Alice set out to churn butter. They took turns turning the crank, lifting the lid of the boxy metal churn to see how near it was to becoming butter. Nero, the farm dog, watched from his spot in the cob basket by the stove. Dry corncobs helped heat the kitchen and provided a soft spot for Nero's nap. They rustled as Nero rolled over, stretched and snored. When the butter was done, Bernie and Alice rinsed it with cool water and worked it with a butter paddle. Alice pressed it into two round molds. "We did a good job, didn't we, Bernie?" Alice said.

"Yes," Bernie admitted. "But I wasn't too excited about spending all day making butter."

Alice laughed. "I don't suppose, but at least you're not in the kitchen hopping through horse manure!"

Bernie smiled a little bit. "I'll go check on Min," he offered. He added with a whisper, "Do you think Pa is ever going home?"

Pa was settled in the front room, reading under the dim light of the kerosene lamp. "Alice," he said, "Come review my letters." Alice sighed and slid beside him on the couch. Minnie tutored Pa in reading and business writing. Now he read well, but continued to struggle with his writing. "Minnie, why did you have to catch a cold today, of all days?" Alice mumbled to herself. She didn't have Minnie's patience for tutoring. Pa was often grouchy and frustrated when the words didn't come easily. This evening he was sure to be in an even worse mood.

"What are you writing, Pa?" Alice asked.

"A note to Minnie," he replied.

Alice leaned closer to the light. The paper read, "Minnie, I hope you feel better tomorrow. The kitchen is bright. Bernie and Alice have worked hard. Pal is well and the storm is over. Pa."

"It's good, Pa!" Alice said. Pa smiled with pride, and Alice warmed. Perhaps it hadn't been such a bad day after all.

Confirmation Class of 1910.
Alice - middle row, third from left.
Martin - middle row, second from right.

Chapter 7

The bitter winter warmed to a glorious spring. Tiny seeds burrowed deep in the rich earth sprouted hearty and green in the summer sun. Crops were harvested in the Fall and another cold winter set in. And another year passed. Winter winds raced across the snowy farms again as Alice blew out fifteen candles on her birthday cake.

"Oooh, another one!" Alice squealed as Bernie pulled a brightly wrapped package from behind his back.

"Not as expertly wrapped as our sister's, I'm afraid," Bernie teased.

Minnie bristled good-naturedly. "So I guess you'll be skipping cake then, Bernie?" Minnie smiled.

Alice looked around the table lovingly. It had been a long time since they'd all been together. Pa leaned comfortably on the buffet at the end of the table, lazily smoking his long cigar. Ma bounced baby Mildred on her knee, trying to entertain the antsy one-year-old with a sugar cookie. Ma always seemed frazzled with Phoebe, Orville, Evelyn, and now baby Mildred to look after. Ma's recent visits to the house had been hurried and tense. But today, Alice thought, she looked like she was enjoying herself.

"Al, open it! Let me help!" Phoebe offered, bouncing up to the table to tear at the pink paper.

"Easy," Bernie cautioned. "It might be breakable, you know. There might be a big old chicken egg in that box."

Phoebe's face fell. "But that's not a very exciting gift, Bernie," she scolded, her tiny hands on her hips.

Everyone laughed and Alice paused to enjoy the sight of everyone's smiles. "The box, Al," Phoebe reminded her.

"Oh, Bernie, it's gorgeous!" Alice exclaimed, holding up a petite hand mirror. Etched on the gold back was the profile of an elegant young lady. It twinkled in her hand.

The group murmured approval as Bernie beamed, pleased at his shopping skills. Alice turned the mirror over and stopped in surprise when she caught her reflection. Her cheeks were pink with excitement and her dark eyes flashed against the green blouse that was Minnie's gift to her. Minnie had wound Alice's glossy black hair into a bun, securing it with a matching emerald ribbon and had lent her a black crepe skirt that reached all the way to the floor. With a start, Alice realized that her reflection was that of a young woman rather than a little girl. Looking down the table at Pa, she read the same thought in his black eyes. Her real mother, they both were thinking, would have been proud. Alice imagined that beautiful Emma would have smiled, hugged her tightly and would have joined Pa in singing, "Happy Birthday, dear daughter." Alice had a sudden pang of grief that no amount of birthday cake could erase.

It was a month later before Alice got to wear her birthday present from Pa and Ma. The crisp, white dress with embroidered lace and creamy sash lay gently folded for this special occasion. Today, she would be confirmed in church. Even the weather recognized today was special.

"Out of bed sleepy-head," Minnie encouraged. "Look outside, Al. The sky is going to be clear, with no rain to splash on your white dress after all!"

"Is everything ready for the reception, Min?" Alice asked.

"All ready," Minnie assured her. "That is if you can get through the church ceremony without fainting."

Alice smiled. She was confident she was ready for the quizzing that the pastor would give them in front of the church congregation. "I know my lessons backwards and forwards," she assured Minnie. "Which is more than I can say for Frosty! We may need to prop him up!"

It wasn't long before she slipped into the perfect white dress, savoring the feel of fine, linen cloth. She fastened each tiny pearl button and enlisted Minnie's help to loop the sash so it knotted at the waist in a little rosette. Her hair was swept back and finished off with a wide white bow.

"Perfect," Minnie said. Alice pinned a silver broach to her high lace collar and checked her reflection one more time. Impulsively, she grabbed Minnie in a tight bear hug. "Goodness!" Minnie exclaimed. "What was that for?"

"For helping me on my special day," Alice replied, her cheeks pink with excitement.

Since she had to be there early Bernie drove her to church alone. As they pulled up, he said, "It looks like everyone is meeting in the back room. You go on. I'll see to the buggy." He smiled broadly as she stepped down. "You'll do fine, Al."

"Thanks, I know, I will," Alice replied. Today she felt like she could conquer the world. She gathered her skirt so it didn't get caught in the door, and ran headfirst into Frosty.

"Oh, sorry!' she cried. "I didn't see you! Too occupied arranging my ruffles, I guess."

Frosty just stared. Already flushed, Alice's cheeks blushed even more.

"What?" she demanded. "Did I step on your toe or something?" When Frosty didn't answer, she stepped forward and waved her palm in front of his stony face. "Yoohoo, Frosty! Is that fancy starched shirt cutting off your air?"

Frosty refocused. "Sorry, it's just that, well, you look so pretty today."

Now it was Alice's turn to be speechless. That was a strange comment for Frosty. She didn't remember him even thinking anything was pretty, except maybe his horse's coat after he'd brushed her. Alice made a silent note to thank Ma for picking out such a stunning dress.

Frosty grabbed her hand impulsively and kissed her swiftly on the cheek. "I'll show you where we need to meet, Al," he said, leading her down the hall. Alice followed, dumfounded. Yes, this was definitely shaping up to be a special day.

Chapter
8

"Ladies, I'm home from town!" Bernie hollered up the stairs.

"Coming," Minnie replied. She was mid-way down the stairs before Alice caught up, passing her and lunging for Bernie.

"I get it first, Bernie!" she laughed. She grabbed for the newspaper her brother held high over his head.

"Oh, Alice," Minnie said. "Calm down. We'll lay it out on the table and read it together."

Two dark heads bent low over the next installment of the story "My Lady of the South" from The Wenona Index stretched nearly the length of the worn kitchen table.

"My Darling Calvert," Bernie teased. "Hold my hand or I fear I'll faint dead away."

His sisters looked up crossly. Alice snapped. "Go feed the pigs or something, and leave us be."

"Well how about that," Bernie, chuckled on his way out. "I think I do have some pigs to feed."

"Oh Min," Alice squealed as she finished the page. "Jean *does* love Colonel McDonald. She all but says so. I knew it!"

"But she's married to Dunn!" Minnie said. "And Colonel McDonald is so old." A dreamy expression smoothed her face. "When I fall in love he'll be young, tall and handsome. He'll have light blue eyes – no, green like mine - blonde hair and a cute, lopsided smile."

"That's quite a list. I don't think anyone could match up! But while you're at it, why don't you ask for a charming southern accent?"

Smiling, Minnie scooped up the paper. "Yes, an accent would top it right off. We'd better leave the dream world and concentrate on the real world, or we'll never be ready for the Box Social."

Box Socials were always fun. The women and girls packed delicious lunches in pretty boxes and the men and boys bid on them at an auction. The man who won the bid not only got to eat the lunch, but also got to eat it with the lovely lady who made it. Today's Box Social was being held at the new high school, under construction, and the proceeds from the auction would benefit the school.

At the Appleton farm, Mrs. Appleton and Clara argued in the kitchen as Frosty lugged two pails of milk through the back kitchen door.

"But Ma, I'm old enough to stay home by myself, and I'm not interested in the Box Social," Clara whined. "Why would I want to raise money for the high school when I don't even get to go there?"

"Clara," Mrs. Appleton said. "It's up to all of us to support Wenona High and Martin. Your brother, Frosty, is a student there. What will you do here alone?"

"I'll play the piano without any big brothers asking me to be quiet."

"I insist you come with us." It will be fun to be in the park and see all the gaily decorated boxes, not to mention all the wonderful food. I'm glad you enjoy playing the piano, but it will have to rest without you this afternoon. Keep in mind, you might go to high school someday and then you'll appreciate how you helped raise money for the school."

"*That* will never happen," Paul grumbled entering the kitchen and joining the conversation. He rudely bumped past Frosty. Frosty's cheeks blushed red, an angry retort on the tip of his tongue.

"Don't give me that look brother," Paul continued, his eyes narrowing. "You're the only lucky one that gets to go to high school. Those of us who work all day will spend our hard earned money to buy the fancy boxes to keep your school going." He turned abruptly, leaving Frosty slumped in the doorway, still balancing his milk pails.

His mother smiled sympathetically. "Martin, don't pay him any attention. We're happy to support the school." Clara, can you decorate the box for me?"

Clara brightened at the task. "Can I use any of the bits of ribbon I like? Even the extra pearl buttons and scraps of velvet?"

"Yes," Mrs. Appleton replied, kissing Clara's cheek. "I know you're a little young to make a box of your own, but just for fun, let's call this one yours and we'll see what handsome prince buys it."

Clara smile, her piano forgotten.

Buggies, horses and people on foot all converged on the school grounds. Nearly the entire town spread blankets on the grass then strolled under the trees. Alice, Minnie and Bernie searched for the best picnic spot. Anna, a pretty girl from town, swept up and linked her arm with Bernie's. "I made the pink box with the gold ribbon," she said, flashing a bright smile. "It has four pieces of apple pie inside."

Alice giggled as Bernie rattled off questions about the box Anna brought.

"Apple did you say, Anna? And a pink box? Did it have a ribbon?"

Anna just waved her hand lazily and strolled off, leaving Bernie drooling. "Honestly, Bernie," Minnie clucked. "You go plum crazy when you hear the word 'pie'!"

"You're right. And now I'm off to examine each of the boxes and figure out which has the most food. I want to get my moneys worth!" he said, sidestepping a playful slap from Minnie.

Alice scanned the crowd for Frosty's bright hair. When she spotted him among a circle of bows and skirts, she felt a little pang of jealousy. "Goodness," she scolded herself. "Why should I care if Frosty surrounds himself with giggling girls?" Nevertheless Alice smoothed back her hair and walked over to say hello.

It was the end of the day before Alice really got a chance to talk to Frosty alone. The sun inched low in the spring sky and the air chilled as they lounged on their picnic blankets. "You're awful quiet today, Frosty. Anything wrong?" Alice asked.

"Just feeling sorry for myself, I guess."

"On such a happy day? Why? I heard they raised over a hundred dollars for the school."

"That's just it," Frosty explained. "The school. Ma and Clara were arguing, and Paul was giving me a hard time and truth is, I feel terrible that I'm the only one in our family who gets to go to high school. The folks only let me go because they have Paul to help out on the farm."

"Couldn't Paul come to high school if he wanted to?"

"Nope. Art and Ansfred have struck out on their own and Pa can't farm the place by himself. So Paul is stuck."

"Why were your mother and Clara arguing?"

"Clara didn't want to come to the social. She wanted to stay home and play her piano. I'm sure, deep down she knows that she won't be coming to high school when she gets older either."

Alice's eyes widened in surprise. "Why not?" she asked.

"Al," Frosty said, his eyes solemn. "It's not like your house where you've got Bernie and the hired men to go help with the farm work and you and Minnie to do the house work. At our house, my older sister will soon be married, and then there's just Clara left to help Ma. I think Pa bought her that piano to make up for the fact that she won't get to go to high school."

Alice sighed. Until now, she hadn't thought of what it must take for her Pa and Ma to send them all to school. And she wasn't sure what she would do if she didn't have the chance to come. High School showed her that there was a huge world out there to explore – beyond these fields and beyond this county. She meant to get out there and see it. Alice, lost in her dreams and Frosty, lost in his sadness, felt a tugging on the blanket.

"Hop up," Minnie said. "Time to get going."

Bernie waddled over to join them, making no attempt to pick up the blanket. "My stomach is too full to budge," he groaned. "That second piece of pie put me over the edge."

"Pie would have been nice," Frosty sighed, while the others laughed.

"Oh, Frosty," Bernie consoled. "How were you to know that Olga's fancy box contained three slabs of the heaviest fruitcake on earth?" Grinning, he added, "Plus you got to eat lunch with her. I'm sure she made you eat every last crumb." Al and Minnie giggled as Frosty flopped back on the blanket, holding his belly.

Two lanky men headed their way across the grass. "Who is that with Gust," Bernie wondered aloud, all eyes following his. Gust and the stranger waved. "Hey, that must be Emil, the new hired man from Sweden," Bernie said. "Pa says he's working out at his place."

"Hello everyone," Gust greeted the group. "I wanted to introduce you to Emil."

They stood up to shake hands with the stranger. Alice started to ask him a question, but noticed that he wasn't looking at her. Emil only had eyes for Minnie. As he spoke to Minne, he flashed a charming lopsided smile. "So nice to meet you," he said with a rhythmic Swedish accent. His bright green eyes were a perfect match for Minnie's. Alice and Frosty shared a sideways look, both thinking that they'd never seen Minnie's face so sunny.

"Look sharp, Alice!" Mildred whispered. "Don't let them catch you daydreaming!'

"Calm down, Mildred, no one was looking. And I wasn't really daydreaming, just admiring," Alice said.

Peeking out of the kitchen of the elegant Scott home, Alice and Mildred looked like timid rabbits. They had been hired to help serve a wedding in the splendid manor west of town. It was the first time either girl had been inside the house and today it was an absolute wonder.

The dining room shimmered with white candles on glittering silver candlesticks. Candleglow highlighted polished glass doors and gleaming waxed wood. The rich buffet, glistened with delicate candies and sticky sweets. An exquisite wedding cake adorned with lilies, crowned the display.

Mildred's eyes followed Alice's to the cake. "We'd better keep an eye on that," she said. "If it slips to the floor, we're in for it."

At the sound of cheery voices coming up the walk, the girls straightened their black skirts and stood tall in their starched white blouses. Alice's curiosity got the best of her. She craned her neck to sneak a peek at the carved staircase where the bride, flushed and sparkling, began her descent. The lovely bride floated rather than stepped down the stairs, gracefully running her hand along the polished banister. Alice's eyes followed as she turned into the ornate living room. The young women settled on a tufted window seat and was surrounded by clucking sisters and aunts. They whispered and giggled as they adjusted her veil and straightened her dress. Late morning light streamed in behind the group, illuminating the queen-like bride. Alice stood captivated. Mildred jarred her with a pinch on the arm. "Alice, let's get going! The guests are here!

The wedding ceremony went quickly, while Alice and Mildred prepared plates in the kitchen. They scurried all afternoon, serving foamy punch, colorful fruits and exotic nuts. Alice was amazed at the main dish. Sweet crackers had been woven into baskets, filled with chicken salad and topped off with candy ribbons that were edible! The guests gasped with delight when they discovered that the baskets tasted as good as the chicken salad inside. The china gleamed against the lace tablecloths, the grand house was full of laughter, and Alice was proud to have helped serve such a meal.

Finally, the last guest left and the kitchen was clean. Alice slumped on a chair and loosed her tightly wrapped hair. If felt good to shake it loose. Having an extra job was hard but she liked being in town. Minnie could get by on the farm without her every once in awhile and it was good to earn her own money. She fingered the coins in her pocket. With enough of these, she thought, there were so many places she could go. She might even live in a big city, like Chicago, or New York. She didn't want to live on a farm all her life. Minnie seemed content, even happy about that possibility. Knowing Minnie, she was probably humming in the kitchen right now, dreaming about serving Emil dinner. Alice wanted her own job. She wanted to buy fancy clothes, ride a train and stroll down Michigan Avenue.

"Day dreaming again?" Mildred said, plopping down beside her.

"I guess so," she replied. "I was just thinking about Minnie and Emil living on the farm…"

"Ahh…the wedding made you think of them? I'll bet they're married before the year is out."

Alice glanced at Mildred, solemnly. "Do you think so?"

"Sure! They've been sweet on each other for months now. I've been daydreaming too – about wedding dresses. Did you notice the bride's gown? I'll bet the lace was imported from France."

"Yes, it was beautiful, but not as impressive as you could make, Mildred." Mildred's reputation as a seamstress crossed three counties. She had taken two years of sewing classes in Varna and had a waiting list of ladies who needed her services.

Mildred smiled. "Thanks, Alice. I know this sounds like bragging, but I agree with you. I think I could make a dress that's even more gorgeous. Maybe I'll get to practice on Minnie's."

Alice winced. If Minnie got married, that would change everything. Better to not even think about it.

"Hey, Mildred," she said, quickly changing the subject. "Let's go check out the spring styles at Heflin's Store. We have our pockets full of money now…I think we need new hats!"

The girls at the back of Heflin's Store,
Alice in the white blouse.

Chapter 10

It was summer and Alice's hair flapped behind her like crow's wings as Mildred accelerated her shiny new automobile. They raced down the country road, dust billowing behind them. Weeds swirled as they passed and the fields blurred. Mildred careened into the lane and screeched to a stop. "Wow! What a terrific ride!" Al exclaimed as both girls caught their breath. Your new car is beautiful. Thanks so much!"

"Thank *you* for taking a spin with me." Mildred said, patting the steering wheel. "I'd be happy to pick you up for next Wednesday's Luther League meeting if you want. A singer from Augustana is going to perform. Convince Minnie to come too. She'd love it."

"I'll ask, but she'll probably spend the evening with Emil." Alice hopped out of the automobile, waved to Mildred, and rushed into the house.

"Min!" she cried. "Did you see Mildred's amazing new auto?" Alice called her sister's name and found her sitting on the parlor settee, staring at her hands. "Minnie," Alice said, "is something wrong?" Alice nestled in beside her sister. Minnie's face was as white as school board chalk.

"Min, tell me, what is it?" Alice asked.

"Emil left for Sweden," Minnie whispered.

"For a visit, right?"

"No, for good. He said he'd always planned to visit America for just a little while, then go back home."

The spark that had brightened Minnie's eyes for the last year had vanished. Alice searched for something to say that would ease a broken heart, but no words came. She slid her hand over Minnie's and squeezed tightly.

Minnie sighed deeply, looked into Alice's eyes and said, "I've made a decision. I'm going to Moline to live with Aunt Betty."

"What? Minnie, you're doing what? Why?"

"I'm going to live at Aunt Betty's. I'll get a job there." She added softly, "Alice, you know I can't stay here forever. What's to keep me now? I need to get off on my own."

Hot tears fill Alice's eyes. She pleaded with her sister. "*I'm* a reason to stay here! I need you – we all need you."

"No, Al," Minnie said, putting her arms around Alice and stroking her hair. "You'll get along fine without me. You need to be the woman of the house for awhile." She gently lifted Alice's chin. "Besides, think of the adventures we can have when you come to visit." Al managed a little smile in spite of herself.

"Really? Do you think Pa will let me take the train by myself? Oh," she said, "speaking of Pa, have you told him?"

Minnie dropped her gaze. "No. He's coming by tonight, so I guess I'll tell him then."

"He won't like it."

"I know," Minnie replied with determination. "But I'm going."

The following week, Alice tried to convince Minnie to

go to Luther League with her after all. "Too much pack-
ing, Al," she said.

Alice settled soberly in the church pew next to Frosty.
Frosty leaned over as soon as they sat down.

"So, is it true that Minnie is going to live in Moline?"

"Yes. Bernie and I are taking her to the train tomorrow."

"What will she do there?"

"Aunt Betty got her a job with Veeley's, part of the
John Deere family. Now shush, I think the singer is about
to begin." Alice didn't have the heart for tonight's music,
but she didn't have the stomach for any more of Frosty's
questions.

"I heard your Pa took it pretty hard," Frosty whispered, just as a pretty girl in a striking blue dress entered
the front of the church.

Alice barely heard the soprano's opening notes. Pa
had definitely taken it hard when Minnie announced she
was leaving. He'd stomped around the kitchen balling his
leathery hands into fists. At one point he'd forbidden her
to go. But Minnie stood her ground. With Bernie and Alice's help, Pa finally gave up his arguments.

Last night, Alice walked through the parlor and found
her father in the near dark. He stood in front of a portrait
of Bernie, Minnie and Alice as young children. Though
Alice couldn't remember posing for the photograph, she
knew that Pa had taken them into town for that portrait
right after their real mother had died. She always wondered why it had been so important to have their picture
taken right then.

"Pa," she had whispered. "Is everything all right?"
He turned, his dark eyes glistening in the kerosene lamp
shadows. He cleared his throat and said, "Bound to happen, I guess, things changing. You'll be the woman of this

house now, Alice. Sometimes I know I've been too hard on you. You remind me so much of your mother. I'll admit it has pained me, at times, to see so much of her in you." He straightened his back. "All grown up, you girls. She would be proud." Without another word, he strode briskly through the front door.

At the sound of wild applause, Alice snapped back to the present. The soprano had finished her first song and Frosty was nearly hopping out of his seat. "Wasn't she fantastic, Al? What a voice!"

Alice listened more closely to the rest of the concert and was captivated by the Swedish melodies. "It would be wonderful to sing like her," she thought. I wonder if I could learn that at Augustana?"

After the concert, Frosty and Alice joined the rest of the group for sugar cookies and fruit drinks. "There she is," Frosty said excitedly. "Let's introduce ourselves." Before Alice could protest, Frosty steered them towards the singer. "Hello, I'm Frosty Appleton," he began, "and this is Alice Crone. We're very pleased to meet you."

The young woman turned their way and extended a slender hand. "Nice to meet you also," she replied. "I'm Linda Johnson."

"Alice's sister is moving to Moline tomorrow."

"Really?" said Linda, turning towards Alice. "She'll love it there. It's an exciting city. She should visit Augie. It's right next door in Rock Island, and is such a beautiful campus. I would be happy to show her around if you'd like to give her my address."

"How kind of you," Alice stammered, overwhelmed by the woman's generosity. Frosty poked a pencil and paper into the singer's hand, and Alice thanked Linda for her offer. It would be nice for Minnie to have a friend in her new home. Minnie at a new home...hundreds of miles away! Alice's lip trembled as she realized how lifeless the farm would feel without her sister.

"Well then," Linda said. "Tell your sister to look me up when she starts her new life." Alice mumbled a reply and wondered if her heart felt sick because Minnie was leaving, or because she wished she was going too.

Alice on the left, Minnie on the right, Alma Crone in the middle.

Chapter 11

For the hundredth time that day, Alice stretched her aching arms over her head, pinning back her reluctant hair. "OK," she thought, hands on her hips. "Lunch is packed for the men to pick up and take to the field. I need to finish the washing and make a batch of biscuits for dinner." She sighed and thought how much easier – and more fun – chores had been when Minnie was here. Her sister would have actually enjoyed baking a pie for the minister's Sunday dinner. Alice wrinkled up her nose, remembering how many times she'd had to roll out the lumpy crust to get it just right. Minnie's always came out perfect the first time.

"Hi, Al," Bernie greeted, screen door banging behind him as he ran in from the porch. "No time to chat, we're running behind. I'll just grab lunch and be off." He swept up the big basket and headed back outdoors. "Oh, I almost forgot, Pa brought over this week's Index. It's on the table in the parlor. He said he's heading into town later today, if you need anything."

Alice fixed a hurried lunch and ate as she read the lat-

est news. "I'll just have time to write Minnie a quick letter," she thought, digging for a tablet and pencil.

Dear Minnie,

*I hope this letter finds you well. Pa is here and he, Bernie
and the other men have been in the fields all day. He said he'd be
stopping by town, so I'll have him send this letter to you.*

*I have been busy tending to the farm while you've been gone
and trying to help Ma with the children. Pa is very anxious
about Ma's health. She always seems tired and sad. The five
kids are quite a handful! Harry just turned six months old and
Mildred and Evelyn play with him like he's a little doll. Phoebe
tries to help and Orville too, when he's not working with Pa.*

*There's not much news from the Index other than a big sale
on linens at Hoge, Monsor and Company. Kreider's Hardware
is advertising Artic Ice Cream Freezers – doesn't that sound
good on a hot summer day? And Bert Lambourn's Grocery is
staying open until 8:00 p.m. these days. Bernie says uptown is
so busy it's hard to find a free hitching post for your horse. The
new autos take up so much room. They opened up a new library
named after Francis Bond, who donated the money. Phoebe and
I visited and checked out books (I had to shush her a little bit).
It has rows and rows of books and quiet spots to read and study.
We're all so proud of it – I can't wait to show it to you!*

*I'm sorry I haven't been able to visit yet. I sure want to!
When the harvest is over, I should be able to get away. We are
butchering at the end of the month, so we'll have fresh bacon
and ham for the Crone Reunion picnic. It will be a lot of work to
put all the meat up in the cellar for the winter, so I hope Ma feels
good enough to come over and help. I do worry about her.*

*Frosty went to the County Fair in Henry and he said the
horse and buggy races were wild. They had bareback riding too,
and one rider's horse bolted clean out of the corral. The rider*

was bucked off, and Frosty thought he was killed. Mildred went too. She said they had the most beautiful carousel she'd ever seen. She and Perle rode on it three times.

I'm making biscuits, Min, and they are hard as clay compared to yours. I'd better get them in the oven. Greet Aunt Betty for me. I miss you very much. I'll bet you're having all kinds of amazing adventures in the city! I can't wait until I'm old enough to leave all this farm work.

Your Loving Sister,
Al

Summer passed quickly for Alice. The days started before the sun was peeking over the fields and ended long after it had bowed its head for the night. She nearly fell asleep rocking on the front porch at dusk, listening to Bernie and the farm hands banter and joke. Lightning bugs filled the fading sky with comforting flickers. Alice cherished the few letters she received from Minnie. They appeared to be cheery, but Alice could read the loneliness between the lines. The visit they had hoped never happened. Alice now needed to watch the children more and more frequently. Ma was getting worse.

Christmas crept up on Alice that year. Autumn had been warm and mild, and it didn't feel like winter until it was time to chop down the Christmas tree. Husking the corn had been the longest chore, though many neighbors had pitched in and they'd finally stored all the corn cobs in the corncrib. Sitting at the kitchen table, Alice cut hundreds of patches of flannel to apply to the fingers of the coarse husking mittens the men wore. Removing the corn husks quickly ripped the mittens and Alice's fingers ached from stitching patches late into the night.

Amidst the Christmas preparations, Alice hoped that Minnie would be able to join them at home.

Dear Minnie,

I'm writing a few lines so Bernie can get this to town today. It's bitterly cold but the kitchen is warm as we've been baking Christmas cookies since morning. Phoebe has been in charge of rolling the dough, and her pink cheeks are covered with flour. Evelyn and Mildred have been decorating the cookies, and as you can imagine, the floor is crunchy with red and green sugar. Most of the dried fruit intended for holly leaves has ended up in tiny mouths!

I hope you will be able to come home for Christmas. I realize it is hard to take time from work, but I'm praying you'll be here.

I'm enclosing the most recent Index. Isn't the velvet gown on page two just gorgeous? It says it is made of deep blue with cream lace. The triangle of fur near the hem is so rich! However, it does say that the pelt is skunk, which I wouldn't fancy wearing. Bernie says he'll be happy to trap us a skunk if we'd like to make the dress, but we'll have to skin it ourselves! Same old Bernie.

Ma is not well, Minnie, and no one is sure what's wrong with her. She's frail and tired. There are days when Pa says she doesn't get up from bed. I help watch the children, but there's little else I can do for her. She doesn't speak much, I can tell her condition is wearing on Pa. I don't think he knows what to do. To tell the truth, it's almost impossible for me to keep both houses going and all the kids cared for. I don't write that because I want you to feel badly about being away – I just don't have anyone else to confide in.

I'd better say goodbye. We still have to string popcorn and cranberries for the tree. I miss you. See you at Christmas!
Love, Al

Christmas was sad that year. Minnie did not come home and Ma was not able to get out of bed. The younger children had been so intent on practicing for their Sunday School pageant and making little Christmas gifts they didn't notice the gloom that had settled over Pa, Alice and Bernie. Phoebe had been honored to serve as Santa Lucia, the Swedish Saint in the program. She had worn the wreath crown of candles and her face beamed.

Alice had her share of candles too. Bernie brought in a huge pine tree. She and the children spent hours tying the little candles to each branch. Alice wondered if Frosty could see the glow from his house when it was lit Christmas Eve. Alice bit her lip, wishing her sister could be home.

All in all, it was hard to be *too* sad on Christmas Eve. Alice and Phoebe had spent all day in the kitchen boiling pork and baking thick rye bread that would be dipped in the kettle of broth. There was also potato pork sausage, homemade cheese, fresh butter and the traditional lingon berries. Lutefisk was another Swedish favorite, and Alice could hardly wait to taste the salty Christmas delicacy. Bernie bought the dried lutefisk in long pieces, which were soaked in wood ashes or lye for three weeks. After that the fished soaked in clear water for a few more days before it would be cooked and eaten. Dessert would be a steamed pudding with cream. As they joined hands for a Swedish prayer over the holiday meal, Alice thought they needed God's help now more than ever.

After dinner they moved to the parlor and Pa read the Christmas story from the heavy, leather-bound family Bible. They carefully lit the tiny candles on the tree. Pa and Bernie watched closely to make sure that none of the candles caught the tree on fire. The little girls passed out the few Christmas presents until everyone had one. The children squealed as they opened their dolls and toys. Alice was handed a package that said "Merry Christmas" in Minnie's handwriting. Pa and Bernie watched her closely as she opened the box, carefully nudging the tissue paper inside. She gasped with surprise and held up an ivory-colored handbag, delicately crocheted.

"Aunt Betty made it," Bernie said. "She and Minnie have been working on it for weeks."

"I love it," Alice exclaimed, as she released the dainty rope drawstring and peered inside. It was lined with creamy lace, gently stitched to the crocheted pattern. The purse was long and rectangular, coming to a point at the bottom. It had a starburst design on each side and every corner had a little tassel.

"I can't wait to show it off at church tomorrow morning," Alice said, knowing that love was sewn into every stitch.

Early the next morning Alice held her new purse against the fur robes that Bernie tucked around her in the sleigh. Bernie flicked the reins, speaking gently to the horses, and they slipped off in the quiet, Christmas dawn.

Alice, with watch from her father, 1914.

Alice and friends.

Chapter 12

"That was the best apple pie I've ever eaten," Pa declared, clanking his fork down on his plate and smiling at Bernie's new girlfriend. "You're a good cook, Florence."

Alice glanced around the crowded Sunday dinner table and noticed that Bernie's girlfriend's face turned pink with Pa's praise. Bernie winked at Florence, and Alice was sure he squeezed her hand under the table.

Ma sat silently at the end of the table. Her thin arms, as brittle as twigs, rested absently on the chair. Circles under her vacant eyes accented her white face. Alice had come over early to help prepare this special meal to welcome Florence. Bernie was nervous that they make a good impression. He must really like her, Alice thought, to make such a fuss. Al had twisted Ma's hair into a pretty bun and helped her into a bright crimson dress trimmed with lace. Alice prattled on about the children and news from town, hoping to cheer her, but her lively chatter seemed to have the opposite effect. By the time they were ready to go downstairs to dinner, Ma was exhausted and withdrawn.

Pa also noticed Ma's fatigue. In his hard face, Alice

noticed a wave of anger play across his features. His taut jaw was clenched and his moustache squirmed. When Ma turned her head towards Pa, he leaned forward, hopeful and expectant. His cheeks softened for a moment. But Ma's unfocused eyes passed over Pa with no more interest than if she were watching grass grow. She didn't even seem to recognize him. Al's heart ached for her father. His lip quivered as he cleared his throat. "Florence, it was a pleasure having you with us. Please excuse us a moment. Bernie and Alice, join me in the parlor."

Alice and Bernice were equally puzzled by Pa's command. In the other room, Pa motioned them to sit. Clasping his hands firmly behind his back, he paced.

"Your ma isn't getting better," he began. "I'm not sure if it's the farm work or the children." He cleared his throat again, "maybe just life. The doctor said she's had a nervous breakdown and she needs to be in a hospital for awhile. I've arranged to take her to the hospital in Moline. We leave tomorrow."

Alice was speechless. Bernie found his voice first and spoke for them both. "Is she going to be all right? Are you sure she's not just tired? Maybe with a little bit more rest she'll…"

Pa cut him off. "She's been resting. It hasn't helped. The doctor says this is the best thing, and I have to trust him. I don't know what else to do." Pa shook his head as if finding all of this hard to believe.

"Of course, Pa," Alice said. She'd heard that some people never recovered from a nervous breakdown. She didn't allow herself to think about losing another mother.

Pa eased himself into a chair, his head dropping into his hands. "My dear Agnes," he murmured, "I'm not sure what I'll do without you."

"Now Pa," Alice replied awkwardly, "It will be fine. I'm sure Ma will be fine."

"Yes, that's right," Bernie chimed in. Never remembering a time when she needed to console her father. "Once she's spent a bit of time at that hospital, I'm sure she'll be her old self again."

"Plus Minnie and Aunt Betty will be able to visit her, Ma will feel right at home," Al added.

Pa nodded. "You know, before we were married, Minnie used to bring me notes from her," he said wistfully. Alice remembered Minnie told her that she and Bernie had played messenger between Ma and Pa, delivering notes when they were dating. "Ma was working for the Hodge family at the corner mansion. I would write her letters and Minnie would deliver them to Ma at the back kitchen door. Minnie would always bring back a reply." Pa's voice cracked.

"Pa, she will get better," Alice said, surprising them all with her confidence. "You'll see. She'll pull through."

Ma left. Alice shuttled between the two farms. It felt like she was drowning in children, cooking and housework. Weeks later the first news came from Minnie.

Dear Bernie and Alice,

I have just a few moments to write, I'm sure you're anxious about Ma. I wanted to assure you that she's doing better. When I visited yesterday, she recognized me. A little light has come back to her eyes.

It was good to see Pa when he came to the hospital, though it would have been sweeter under different circumstances. I admitted how terribly homesick I have been and he told me to pack my things and come on home. It was tempting, but I've started a life here and guess I'll stay. I hope to surely be home for a long visit this summer. I wouldn't miss the Streator Fair! Aunt Betty says hello.

Love from your sister, Minnie

Alice closed the envelope with a selfish sigh, sure that she wouldn't be able to leave the farms, even for a visit to the Streator Fair.

Chapter 13

"Phoebe, don't pull that one! That's a carrot, not a weed!" Alice, Phoebe and Orville were weeding and watering the massive garden. Fragile green seedlings sprouted like a carpet against a black floor. They decided they wouldn't be able to keep up with two vegetable gardens this year, so Pa and Bernie had enlarged this one to grow enough for both households.

"I'm taking a break," Orville announced, stretching his back. "Anyone like a drink?" He headed to the water jug under a tree, when something caught his eye. "Alice, there's someone coming on horseback. Riding fast."

Alice stood up and shaded her eyes to get a better look at the dusty road. Her heart pounded. Ma! Something was wrong with Ma. Judging by the dust that kicked up, the rider was at a full gallop. He was tall and lean. She could see he was dressed in work clothes, a simple shirt and trousers. Alice wiped her hands with her apron and pushed back the strands of hair that swirled around her hot face.

Orville and Phoebe stood beside her as they all tried to guess the identity of the mystery rider.

"You know…" Orville started.

"I think…" continued Phoebe.

Alice finished all their thoughts. "Well, I'll be…It's Emil!"

In another few minutes, Emil was hopping off his horse, shyly accepting the happy greetings and muddy attention.

"I just got back and borrowed Gust's horse to ride right over." Emil said, "Where's Min?"

Alice and Phoebe exchanged uneasy looks.

"What, is it? What's wrong?" Emil asked.

Alice sighed. "Emil, Minnie's moved to Moline."

Emil's face registered confusion. "Permanently?"

"Yes," Alice replied glumly, "for good. But she'll be home next week for a visit. You could see her then."

Emil's grinned. "Next week." Eyes twinkling, he continued. "Don't tell her I'm here, I want to surprise her."

Ma came home with Minnie the following week. Still thin and frail, she nonetheless stepped brightly off the train and hugged her children fiercely. Tears rolled down her cheeks as she approached Alice. Taking her hands, she looked Alice squarely in the eye.

"Alice," Ma said kindly. "Thank you." Alice was surprised to feel her own eyes fill. She hugged Ma tight, thankful to have the old her back.

Ma's homecoming was joyous, but having Minnie back home was heaven. The sisters chatted like spring birds catching up on town news. Minnie marveled at how the little children had grown so quickly and how Alice had kept up with it all. Alice delighted in helping Minnie unpack all the beautiful clothes she'd purchased in Moline. She oohed and ahhed over the fine velvets, light satins and frilly lace.

That first night was special for many reasons. Ma, Pa and the younger children were settled at their place and Alice felt a surprising relief. She wasn't sure if it had to do with Ma, Pa and the little kids being a family again, or if it just felt wonderful to have a break from all the extra work. Best of all was having dinner with Bernie and Minnie at their place, just like the old days. Alice knew Minnie would have an extra special memory of this dinner, since Emil planned to surprise her tonight.

"Al, are you daydreaming?" Minnie asked. "I wanted to tell you about my visit with the singing student you met from Augustana. Linda, remember? She gave me a tour of the campus. It is just beautiful!"

An unexpected noise in the barnyard interrupted them. "What's that?" Minnie asked. "It sounds like someone's pulled up with a buggy."

"Hmm...I'm not sure who it could be," Bernie said. With a quick wink to Alice he hopped up from the table, "I'll go look." he added as he headed towards the door.

"Well, let's clear the dishes," Alice suggested briskly. "I've made your favorite dessert tonight, Minnie. Who knows, we might have company joining us."

As they were setting apple crisp and cream on the table, the door opened. Emil stepped into the kitchen first, a little hesitantly, and cleared his throat. Minnie looked up and her face froze. Al watched her sister, waiting for her to burst into joyful tears. Instead, Minnie straightened stiffly.

Meeting Emil's gaze, Minnie said coldly. "What are you doing here?"

Emil blushed as red as raspberries. "It's good to see you, Minnie," he stammered. At her silence, he continued. "I came right over last week, but they said you were in Moline. I heard you would be back tonight, so I didn't write."

Fire spit from Minnie's eyes. "Didn't write? I'll say you didn't write! At the very least, I expected to hear that you'd reached Sweden safely. You didn't even write!"

Emil bowed his head and fingered the hat he held in front of him. Alice could see he was gathering his thoughts. When he raised his eyes to meet Minnie's, he had a determined look. "Minnie, I had my life planned out when I first came to visit America. I wanted to see a bit of the world before I settled into working the family farm in Sweden. I've spent my life working that place, plowing every inch and loving every harvest. I couldn't imagine any life other than watching it grow to be my own. But then I met you, and suddenly going home to the farm just didn't feel right. It was confusing to have my life all planned and then not want it anymore." Emil continued. "So, I did what I thought would work. I packed up and went back to Sweden for good, just as I'd planned. I couldn't write, couldn't think of America for awhile. I needed to make sure the life I was building in Sweden was what I wanted."

Bernie and Alice held their breath. Neither Emil nor Minnie seemed to notice that there was anyone else in the room.

"But it didn't feel right, Min. The harder I worked, the more empty I felt. The more I made myself forget you, the more you crept into my thoughts. When I finally decided I should come back to America, I felt like a new man."

Alice noticed that Minnie's hard, angry face had softened. Tears glistened in Minnie's eyes but she didn't move or speak. She waited.

"And so, Minnie, I returned." Emil cleared his throat and shifted to his other foot. "I came to ask you to marry me, if you'll have me."

Alice was stunned. She wanted to scream with excitement, but Minnie hadn't moved. The silence hung in the air like an unwanted cloud. Finally, Minne spoke. "Why Emil Johnson, that's the most I've heard you speak in all your days. I would be proud to be your wife."

"Well, I'll be," Bernie said. This one is a big surprise! Congratulations!" They finished dessert chatting about their plans. Emil would stay in America, to get started in farming around Wenona. He thought he could be settled into a place by early next year, so maybe they could get married on Minnie's birthday, January 13th.

"That would be a perfect time," Alice agreed. "You'd have time through the winter months to set up housekeeping before spring planting."

Suddenly Bernie stopped the conversation with a question. "Emil, have you talked to Pa?"

"Goodness, Bernie," Emil replied with exasperation. "Did you think I'd ask for your sister's hand without first asking your Pa?"

"Well no," Bernie stammered, "I just thought I'd better check."

"He seemed pleased," Emil said, looking at Minnie. "Though you know it's hard to tell with your Pa. He didn't say a word until I was leaving. Then he shook my hand and said, 'You're a lucky man, Emil. Welcome to the family.'"

Chapter
14

The Wenona Index announced the "Northern Illinois Fair" at Streator, would "rival the great State Fair in Springfield." Bernie and Emil wondered who would win Best of Show in the large livestock competition. Alice was more concerned about which dress she should wear.

"Minnie, don't you think this light blue looks nice with my hair?" she said, holding it up. But I think the rose one compliments my eyes. Which do you like?"

Minnie laughed. "Whatever you think, Al. I've never met anyone who fusses over clothes as much as you do."

"It's the rose, then," Alice said. "When you see the wedding dress that Mildred is creating for you you'll be happy I fuss. She and I have been working on it together. It's going to be gorgeous."

"I hope it's not too fancy," Minnie said. "Keep in mind I told you I want to wear it for many years. It can't be too elaborate."

"Nonsense," Alice huffed. "You can't be married in an old work dress that you wear to feed the chickens. Mildred says that bows are fashionable this year. Last month's

Index had pictures of silk and velvet ones-some even had rhinestone bows!"

Minnie giggled. "Really, Al. I'm not the type to wear rhinestone bows, no matter what the occasion!"

The Fair was the most fantastic event that Alice could remember. She wished Frosty could have come along. He'd had to go with his father to purchase a new team of ponies. He would have loved the fairgrounds. The fastest, most graceful horses paraded through the stadium, red ribbons gracing their tails, their heads held high. "Just once, I'd like to ride on a horse like that," Bernie commented, mesmerized by a shiny black stallion with fire in its eyes.

"And no doubt you'd end up in Sandy Creek! That one can run," Emil joked.

Minnie and Alice spent most of the morning in the Floral Hall. The sign promised "420 feet by 70 feet of kaleidoscopic beauty under one roof." It wasn't wrong. Exotic plants and bright flower arrangements lined the center of the hall. Oil paintings on gilded easels, intricate carvings and remarkable statues were placed in prominent locations.

"Let's have our picture taken before it gets dark," Minnie suggested. A photographer was posing people in a stationary automobile called "No. 1912." The backdrop read, "10 Miles to Streator."

"I'll drive!" Alice remarked, sliding behind the wheel.

"Don't you think I should drive?"

Bernie joked. "After all, I'm the man of the house."

"Nope. I'll have you know Mildred let me drive her car and I did a fine job."

Emil and Minnie piled into the back seat. Bernie climbed in beside Al. "Pray she doesn't crash us" he murmured as the photographer snapped and the light flashed.

Autumn passed as they planned for Minnie's wedding.

Alice and Minnie harvested the huge garden and the cellar grew with hundreds of jars of fruits and vegetables. At Christmastime, Bernie asked Florence to marry him. Alice had loved Florence as a sister, but her heart ached when she thought of how her little family was going different directions.

Minnie's wedding day dawned frosty and freezing. The week's snow had started to melt, and last night it had refrozen into a slick glaze. "It's going to be tough traveling today unless it warms up," Bernie said, as he came back from the barn. Slipping off his gloves, he held his hands up to the stove and shivered. "It is just frigid out there."

Bernie's remarks barely registered with Minnie. With the first ray of sun she had been floating on air. "Min," Alice had groaned from under her warm covers, "Can't we sleep a little longer?"

"No, Alice!" Minnie had said, offended. "There's too much to do! I couldn't sleep another minute, even if I had the time. I'm too excited. Can you believe that later today I'll be Mrs. Emil Johnson?"

Actually, Alice couldn't quite believe it and had grumbled out of bed while Minnie's puttered. Now, she took Bernie's comments a little bit more seriously than Minnie. "Bernie, do you think everyone will be able to make it here for the wedding? It will be terrible if Ma, Pa and the kids couldn't get here. We need Florence and Frosty here to celebrate with us. Emil's brother Enoch is coming all the way from Chicago. If he can't make it, it would be terrible!"

"I know, Alice. We'll just have to hope it melts off. It's not like this is an unlucky day or anything," Bernie said, eyeing Minnie. "Had it been Friday the 13th, no doubt we couldn't hope for better weather, but today we'll be fine." Bernie winked at Alice.

"Very funny," Minnie said, whirling around with her hands on her hips. "I know you thought I was crazy refusing to get married on my birthday, because it fell on Friday the 13th." She was heating up now, waving a wooden spoon at Bernie. "But I'm not taking any chances on starting my married life on an unlucky day."

"OK, I'm convinced," Bernie chuckled. "And I want you to know any day that Emil gets to marry you is his lucky day."

"Thank you, Bernie," Minnie replied, lowering her spoon and planting a swift kiss on his forehead. "Now add some cobs to the fire for me, will you? I'm almost ready to bake my wedding cake." With that, Minnie was back to beating the fluffy Angel Food cake batter.

"Min," Alice said. "I'm not sure I'll have a chance to give this to you later. I have a little wedding gift – something special for you to wear today."

Minnie wiped her hands on her apron and reached for the tissue-wrapped bundle that Alice held out. "Al, you shouldn't have," Minnie said. She gently folded the paper back. Out popped a white bow decorated with a flash of rhinestone buttons. "Oh, no!" she gasped.

Alice laughed until her stomach hurt. "You don't have to use it today, but it will come in handy when you need to dress up that old black cashmere of yours. Wear it with luck, you old married lady."

Traveling was treacherous for the wedding guests. Emil was the first to drive into the frozen barnyard wearing a serious black suit and holding a heavy Bible. "A new Family Bible for us," he explained, his green eyes shining. "To officially record our marriage." Frosty brought Florence, and Ma, Pa and the children came with the minister. The house filled with giggling young voices and grown-up chatter.

It was almost dusk and Enoch still had not arrived from Chicago. Alice had set out candlesticks in the parlor, and now she lit each one. A warm glow spread over the intimate room. "Perfect," she murmured.

"Alice," she whispered. "Can I talk to you a minute?"

"Of course," Alice said. "What is it?"

"Let's sit," Minnie said, motioning to the couch. "Al, you know there's nothing I wanted more than to have you stand up front as my maid of honor. You and Enoch are so special to us." Alice nodded, knowing what was coming. She made her face look happy. "But with Enoch unable to make it, we're in a spot. Would it be all right with you if Bernie and Florence stood up for us?"

Alice covered her disappointment and forced herself to smile. "Of course, Minnie. They'll do a fine job."

The candlelit ceremony was hushed and holy. Minnie asked Pa to do the honor of recording the marriage names and date in the new Bible. After the ceremony, they all enjoyed Minnie's heavenly cake.

"Can I have a second piece?" Frosty asked sheepishly. Everyone laughed, and soon all the kids were also clamoring for seconds. "Emil, I hear you and Minnie are moving onto the Porterfield farm," Frosty said with a mouthful of cake.

"Yes. Minnie and I are starting a whole new life in America," he said happily. Catching Alice's sad gaze, he added, "Alice, you'll have to visit us often."

"I will," Alice said. She took a deep breath and squared her shoulders. "Of course I'll have plenty to do here to get ready," she said. "Since I'll be leaving next year to go to Augustana College."

Frosty choked so hard on his last forkful of cake that Bernie had to clap him soundly on his back. Alice, exchanging a knowing look with Minnie, suddenly had the strength to meet Pa's stare. "I've been accepted, Pa," she said. "I'll be studying music. I can stay with Aunt Betty."

Frosty was the first to break the silence. He pushed his heavy chair away from the table and stood with his glass held high. "I'd like to propose a toast," he said. "To new beginnings." Everyone echoed his sentiments, clinking their glasses and all talking at once. As he sat down, Frosty leaned close and whispered in Alice's ear, "Al, just make sure you come back!"

In Streator, about 1912. Minnie & Emil not married yet,
nor Alice or Bernie.

Chapter 15

Alice scrambled up the steps of Old Main at Augustana College, her leather boots slipping on the stones. She had an hour before her vocal lesson, and was happy to find her favorite spot, the side ledge at the top, unoccupied. She settled her skirts around her, dangling her feet. She loved this view. The front of this yellow stone building and its massive dome faced the Mississippi. Today, the muddy waters wound through the fiery red and orange colors of autumn. For Fall, it was surprisingly warm. The thick slabs underneath her soaked up the sun and were warm to the touch. Alice felt an amazing sense of pride at being a part of this building's history. This stone, she thought, running her hand along its rough ripples, might provide a seat for her children. Perhaps one day her grandchildren, and their children, would sit on this ledge and admire this view.

"Alice! Hey, Alice!" called a cheery voice. She shaded her eyes to see Myrtle waving as she climbed the steps. "I'm headed for a cup of coffee. Want to join me?"

"I'll be right there!" Alice replied, gathering her books. She hopped off the ledge and brushed the backside of her charcoal-gray skirt.

"Look, Al, they're breaking ground for the new library."

"I saw the plans on display in East Hall. Denkmann Library, they say. It's going to be huge."

"We definitely need it. I heard someone say that we had nearly 200 students and 30 professors now."

"I hope we'll still be able to get our favorite table at College Drug," Alice said with a laugh.

Walking with Myrtle reminded Alice of Minnie. She missed her sister. Minnie had settled into married life like a lady's hand slides into a fine leather glove. She adored her new home on the farm. Though they had little furniture and just a few kitchen things, Minnie kept it spotlessly clean. Alice felt right at home when she pulled up to Minnie's kitchen table with a cup of coffee. "What were you saying, Myrtle?" Alice asked, pulling herself back to the present. She'd been so lost in her daydream that she hadn't noticed the handsome young men that had joined them.

"I want to introduce you to Conrad," Myrtle repeated. "He was in one of my classes last semester. Conrad Bergendoff, Alice Crone."

"Pleased to meet you, Alice," the man said in his soft, whistling voice.

"Nice to meet you too."

"Are you from around here?" Conrad asked.

"No, I'm from Wenona, in Central Illinois."

"Wenona," he repeated. "I think I remember a seminary student who once spent the summer in Wenona."

"That could be," Alice said excitedly. "Our church has Swede School every summer and an Augie student comes to teach. It's amazing that you've heard of my hometown."

"He mentioned what a friendly place it was." Conrad's eyes twinkled. "I also remember him saying he ate a lot of pie that summer."

"That's our town!" Alice laughed.

Alice had looked forward to her life at Augustana for a year. Bernie and Florence married in April, after Minnie. After that Alice felt like she was the only one not moving on with life. Music had always been her passion, and she decided she would like to teach it. "You'll make a great teacher," Frosty had said. "Of course I'm not sure how you'd handle it if you got an ornery fella like me in your class."

"I wouldn't worry about that," Alice had replied haughtily. "I can't image you carrying a tune well enough to even be *in* a music class!"

She missed Frosty's jokes. Today was Saturday, and she knew if she was home she'd be heading to town for supplies. She would no doubt have run into Frosty.

"Myrtle, I better stop by Aunt Betty's on the way. She's expecting me."

"That's fine. It's such a gorgeous day I feel like I could walk for hours. Conrad, will see you later," Myrtle said as the girls continued down the sidewalk.

Aunt Betty bustled in from the kitchen when the girls came through the door. "Guess what, Al? Minnie telephoned you!"

Aunt Betty had just installed a telephone. It still seemed like a strange idea to talk to someone through a box.

"Ohh!" Alice said excitedly. "I'll call her right back."

Hearing Minnie's voice brought back a flood of memories from home. "How are classes going?" Minnie asked, her voice crackling through the line.

"Just fine. Music education is my hardest. Myrtle and I are heading to the drug store to study for a test on Monday."

"And I'm just trying to clean my messy house!" Minnie replied.

"Oh, Min, your house is always scrubbed beyond clean – I'll bet you've got fresh bread baking too. Wish I was there!"

"I wish you were here too. But remember, Al, you've got a great chance to meet new people and learn exciting things. Soak it all up."

"But I miss home so much."

"I know. Believe me, I know. We'll see you soon, though. You go study hard."

"Ok, love to everyone there."

"Same to you and Aunt Betty," Minnie replied as she hung up.

As the girls walked the short distance to the drug store, Alice couldn't decide if it had made her feel better or worse to talk to Minnie. A few minutes later, when they were settled at the back table, life was good again. Alice blew gently on her five cent cup of coffee. "Myrtle, I've been noticing your new hairdo all day," She said. "What did you do to it?"

"Oh, you like it? I saw it in a magazine. You braid it in two braids and wind it up into a little...well kind of a..."

"A hill?" Alice offered.

Myrtle giggled. "OK, a hill. The ends of the braid are loosened to make softer twists at the top, with little loops of hair to the side."

"It looks really stylish. Do you think it would work for my hair too?"

"We'll give it a try. Let's finish studying and go back to your aunt's to put it up."

Later, at Aunt Betty's, the two girls struggled with Alice's unruly hair until their laughter forced the older woman to find them fresh hankies to wipe their eyes. "I give up," Alice announced. "My friend Frosty would say this heap on my head is just one step above a hen's nest!"

"You might be right," Myrtle said, critically eyeing Alice's hair from all sides. "You have a pretty good 'hill' too!"

"More like a coal dump," Alice said.

"What's a coal dump?" Myrtle asked.

"In Wenona, at the coal mine, they separate the black coal from the slag rock, then haul away the coal. The slag is piled up. Each little town that has a mine also has a slag pile, or coal dump. Wenona's is as big as a little mountain." Admiring her hair in the hand-held mirror, she continued, "and I can see the resemblance!"

"Al, I know we can get it right. Then we'll march right down to Philleo's Portrait Studio and have our picture taken."

"Huumpf!" Aunt Betty commented from the other room. "The thought of going out in public like that!" The girls giggled until they slumped on the couch to catch their breath.

It was soon spring on the Old Main steps. Alice and Myrtle breathed in the fresh air. "What a good idea, Alice, to have our pictures taken on the steps before we leave for the summer."

Alice impulsively hugged her friend. "I want a picture so I can remember you when I'm home. Let's each stand on a step so Aunt Betty can get us all in."

"Smile girls!" Aunt Betty called out. Myrtle turned obligingly towards the camera but Alice turned, captured by the sigh of the mighty river, ever flowing, winding its way home.

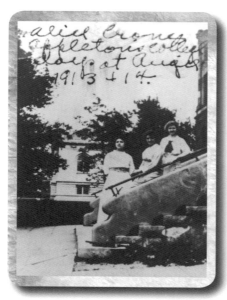

*Alice and friends
on Old Main steps,
Augustana,
1913 or 1914.*

*Alice studying at
Augustana.*

*Alice and Myrtle,
while students at
Augustana.*

Chapter 16

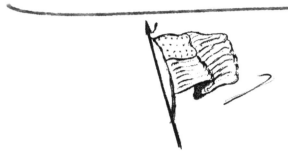

"What a perfect night for a band concert in the park," Alice thought as she brushed out her hair. She had been home from college for over two months but hadn't been to one of the weekly concerts yet. At the sound of horse hooves thudding in the barnyard she peeked out the up-stairs window. The team snorted and pranced their way to the back door. Frosty hopped out and cleared the steps in one stride. "Come on in!" Alice called before he could even knock.

Creaking open the screen door, Frosty reached down to pet a chubby cat who was determined to beat him in-side. "I'll be ready in a minute," Al called down.

"Take your time! Hey, the house looks great. I came over once while you were gone and it was like ghosts lived here."

"I know what you mean," Alice said, as she came into the kitchen. "It was kind of creepy to move back in."

"So how does it feel now?" Frosty asked.

"Pretty empty. It will be good to get out."

"Well, let's go, the buggy is ready."

There was still plenty of activity uptown as they drove

down Main Street. The stores stayed open later in the summer. They drove past Bremmer's Men's Store and Brayman's Jewelry. There were two different hardware stores in town. Alice waved to the minister's wife coming out of Heflin's Department Store and smiled at Mrs. Nelson as they passed by.

"I missed our uptown," Alice said. "Rock Island and Moline have more stores, but it's not the same as nodding to everyone you know when you shop."

"I know what you mean," Frosty replied. "I come to town to pick up supplies, but mostly to see people and hear the news. This week, everyone has been talking about that assassination over in Europe that has the whole continent feuding."

"I read about that in the Index," Alice added. "The Archduke of Austria, and his wife. That's terrible."

"It was just like a line of dominoes, you push one over and it knocks over the rest. Russia, Germany, France, Britain – everyone is wrapped up in a war. Crazy, isn't it?"

"Well, it's a whole ocean away from here, so nothing we have to worry about in Wenona. Frosty, look at all the people uptown tonight! Business must be good on Main Street."

"Oh Al, I meant to tell you that I stopped in Downey's Drug Store the other day and they already have all their school supplies out. Thought you might need to stock up on notebooks and pencils for Augie." Frosty pulled in on the north side of Main Street and slowed by a hitching post. He hopped out, tied up the horses, then came around to help Alice down from the buggy.

"Frosty, about those school supplies," she said. "I've decided not to go back to Augustana."

"Really? How come?"

"I loved music and I had fun living with Aunt Betty and meeting new friends, but I don't think I'm cut out to be a teacher. I was awful homesick. I don't know if this is where I always want to be, but Rock Island just didn't feel like home."

"Well, I'm happy you're back," Frosty said, giving her arm a squeeze. "We'll be able to see each other all the time."

"Well, not as much as you think," Alice said.

Frosty raised his eyebrows. "What do you mean?" he asked.

"I'm starting to work at Heflin's Dry Goods store on Monday."

"Wow! That's great, Al. But it will be quite a trip in from the farm each day."

"I'm going to move into town and stay with Aunt Tildy. It'll be closer, and it's too lonely for me out in the country. Like you said, it does feel like a ghost house when I'm out there all by myself."

Frosty slipped off his hat and slapped it on his leg. "I swear I've heard it all! It sure is good to have you home," he said, a sparkle in his blue eyes. Alice sighed as they strolled over to the band concert. She imagined moving again, starting over in town and living with yet another aunt. Why, she wondered, is "home" so hard for me to find?

Alice had shopped at Heflin's many times, but it all looked different on her first day of work. How would she ever find all the buttons, linens, socks and shirts? Plus learn all the prices? The store was packed to the tall ceiling with merchandise. Shoes, boots and coveralls occupied the bottom shelves. Shirts, stockings, undergarments and material crowded the middle shelves. Hardest to reach, hats, towels and more bolts of fabric towered on top.

"Alice! Welcome!" Jenny greeted her, linking her arm in Al's. "Let me give you a quick tour and introduce you to the other girls." In no time Alice was bustling around the store, finding size 10 overshoes for Mr. Adamson and reaching for a spool of lavender ribbon for Mrs. Monser. The three other girls and Mr. and Mrs. Heflin made her feel right at home.

She quickly got in the habit of noticing when the bell on the door tinkled. This time she was high on a ladder, wrestling down a bolt of cream muslin. "Minnie!" she exclaimed, "Perle! What are you two doing here?" She descended the skinny ladder and smoothed her black skirt.

"We've brought lunch," Minnie said, holding up a woven basket with a clean towel laid neatly across the top.

"Jenny said you'd have time about 12:30," Perle said. "So we thought you could join us across the street on the picnic tables."

"What a great idea. Now that I think about it, I'm absolutely starving."

Minnie and Perle's chatter was a delight. "How is it living at Aunt Tildy's house?" Perle asked.

"I love being in town. I can walk up to the store and Aunt Tildy enjoys my company."

"Do you miss being out at the farm?" Minnie asked.

"I haven't much thought about it," Alice replied. "I miss the wide open fields. I felt like I could see forever out there. I think there are more stars out there too," she added, laughing.

Her first day ended with another surprise, as Frosty pushed the door and jingled the bell. "Hi Al," he said, nodding to Jenny and the other girls. "I was over at Scott's Lumber Yard picking up some new boards for the hay rack. Thought I'd stop in and see how your first day was going."

"It has been wonderful. I was a little nervous at first, learning the layout and everything else, but now I'm getting the hang of it."

"Suppose I should buy something?" Frosty asked in a low tone. "To make it official?" He winked mischievously at Alice and with a raised voice. "I'm looking for a new pair of underdrawers. It appears as if Alice is a little embarrassed to help me. Would one of you other ladies be able to lend me some assistance?" The shop girls giggled and Alice blushed as red as a radish. Slapping Frosty on the shoulder, she grabbed his arm and steered him toward the door.

"Get out of here before you get me fired," she whispered, pushing him out the door. Frosty removed his straw hat and swept it in a low bow on his way out.. "As you wish, Ma'am. I'll come back for my underdrawers another day."

"On my day off, please!" Alice replied, laughing as she pulled the door closed.

Aunt Tildy's House.

Chapter 17

Summer turned quickly to autumn. One evening Alice and Mildred huddled on Aunt Tildy's front porch swing, bundled up against the chill.

"Time passes differently here in town, Mildred," Alice said. "Have you noticed that? At the farm I always knew what time of the year it was by looking at the height of the corn, or the thickness of the horse's coats. Here in town the weather is the only clue."

"I know what you mean," Mildred replied, her high button shoes lazily propelling the swing back and forth. "When I'm living with a farm family, the rhythm of the house turns around the seasons. It's not like that as much in town." Mildred was renowned across the county for her superb sewing skills. She traveled from family to family making their spring or fall wardrobes, living with each family for a week or two until the job was done. Each family furnished her with a room, meals, materials for the clothing, and additional pay.

"Alice," Mildred said, "Can you believe how the war in Europe has spread? Even boys from the U.S. might be going over."

Alice sighed. "It's horrible, all the soldiers that are dying. And for what?"

"Yes, and I heard that..."

"Let's not discuss it, Mildred," Alice interrupted. "I told Frosty I don't even want to think about it. Anyway, I'm sure it will all be over soon."

"O.K., Al, let's change the subject."

"Well, did I tell you what Orville talked me into?"

"No, but whatever it is, I won't be able to help," Mildred replied, laughing. "I'm all too familiar with Orville's schemes!"

"He's organizing a spook house at church for Halloween. The Luther League is sponsoring it and he's in charge. Come be a witch with me! It will be fun!"

Mildred laughed. "I'm sure I'll be busy that day, but I'll be happy to help with the costumes. I'm not very good at cackling and swatting people with a broom."

"Oh, I can do that part just fine," Alice said, chuckling.

On Halloween night, no one would have suspected that the dark dungeon room was really the church basement. "I hardly recognized Orville," Alice said to Frosty. "That powdered face and those vampire teeth fooled me!"

"But that slick black hair is just the same," Frosty replied, loud enough for Orville to hear. "And he's a bossy monster too!"

"I heard that," Orville said, offended. "Someone's got to take the lead around here. Now Frosty, I need you up front. People will start coming soon, and I want them to meet the devil first." Frosty playfully saluted and headed towards the door. Alice admired his bright red outfit. She'd picked out crimson fabric and Mildred had sewn it into a flowing cape with a high collar. "I hope he doesn't poke someone with that pitchfork," Orville worried.

Turning to Alice, he said. "I want you in the kitchen to the right. The other witches will be there stirring the cauldron. And I want to hear lots of cackling!"

Not only was there lots of cackling, there was moaning, howling and screaming. Everyone was nearly hoarse by the end of the night. They gathered for hot cider in the kitchen and all agreed that it had been great fun.

"Three cheers for Orville," Phoebe said. "You did a great job."

"Yes, an especially good job of scaring your own brother and sister," Alice added, with mock disapproval. "I thought poor Harry and Mildred were going to jump out of their skins!"

"But they did add some realistic screaming," Cousin Peddy said, and everyone laughed.

"Alice," Perle asked, "did you make these pralines? They're delicious, what's in them?"

"They're a recipe of Mrs. Heflin's," Alice replied.

"Well Al," said Peddy, munching on the chewy candy, "When Frosty and I are off to war, you'll have to send us some." All conversation stopped. The room was silent.

Frosty shifted uncomfortably, and finally said, "You know, there's a lot of talk about how America has been pulled into the war overseas."

"Yep," Orville added, "Just the other day at Barrett's store, I heard Alphonso say we'd be over there before Christmas."

Peddy chimed in next. "If our country needs us, we gotta go." Slapping Frosty on the knee he said, "We've already talked, haven't we Frosty, about how we'll march right across the Rhineland, kick a few Germans and be back in time for Christmas!"

"Count me in," George said. "They've never seen

fighters like good old American farm boys!"

"I'm going home," Alice announced suddenly.

"I'll walk you," Frosty said, quickly rising to his feet.

"No, thank you," Alice replied icily. "I'd rather go alone." No one spoke as her pointed witch boots tapped angrily towards the door.

Outside, she sucked the cold air into her lungs. It was bad enough that a war was going on. But to hear Frosty and his buddies talk, they couldn't get there fast enough! Apparently, like they all had discussed it, it seemed to be decided. Suddenly everything about this Halloween seemed more frightening.

Chapter
18

"Alice Lydia, come *on!*" Bernie hollered from the car. "If you don't hurry, we'll miss them altogether!"

Inside Aunt Tildy's house Alice struggled to pin her smart new hat over her curls. Finally satisfied with the angle, she slipped on her coat and pulled on leather gloves. Glancing in the mirror, she barely recognized the girl gazing back at her. Her skin was pale and pasty. Her eyes were sunken and reminded her of Ma's unfocused gaze before she went to the hospital. Shaking her head, she pinched color into her cheeks and practiced a smile. Today, of all days, she wanted to look lively.

The threat of war swept through America like an ugly storm. Alice watched it with dread, like a thundercloud gathering strength in the distant fields. Shops and dinner tables were all filled with talk of Germany, the Kaiser and America's role. Young men were laughing and brave, leaned back in their chairs bragging how they could win the war, just send 'em over. They urged their buddies to join with them with grins and slaps on the back. Puffed full of pride, anxious to serve their country, they rushed to greet the storm. The thundercloud grew darker. Alice worried that it would swirl away her world any minute. It did. Frosty enlisted and was mustered into service in Lacon on February 28, 1918. Today in less than an hour, she would stand at the train station and wave him off to Fort Leavenworth and to war.

"Al, are you all right?" Bernie asked gently. "We're almost there."

"I'm fine," Alice replied. "I just can't believe it. It's unreal that he should be going so far across the ocean. He's never even left Illinois! I'm afraid it will take a miracle to bring him back home again. I'm not sure such a miracle is possible."

Bernie nodded as they pulled into the train station in Henry. The platform swarmed with exuberant men in uniform and their anxious families. "You're right, Al, many of these men will not be coming back," Bernie said as he guided Alice through the crowd. "But our job today is to see our Wenona boys off with a smile. Can you do that little sister?"

Alice mustered her most convincing grin. "You bet I can," she replied

"That's the spirit, Al. Let's go find Frosty."

Frosty was one of the few men in uniform not wearing his hat. It wasn't hard to see his bright hair in the crowd. "Frosty!" Alice cried above the sea of heads.

"Here I am," he called. He managed to snake his arm through the crowd and pull Alice to his side. "Our boys are near the edge of the station," he said. Settling his soldier's hat on his head, he grinned, "I knew you'd pick out my hair. By golly that bright hair oughta scare a few Germans!" All of a sudden Alice was in the company of familiar faces - Wenona faces, people she cared about. Everyone was chattering. Mothers were pressing last minute packages of cakes and candies into jacket pockets. Fathers were leaning in close, whispering for one last piece of advice. Her cousin, Peddy Nelson, was here, as was John Zimmerman and Clarkson Brown. Alice scanned the crowd for Alphonso Barrett, knowing he was leaving with the other four. "He's loading his pack on the train," Frosty said, reading her mind. "We're all here. We're all ready."

Alice turned towards Frosty and for a minute it felt like just the two of them. Then she heard a whistle blow, and her cheek brushed against the rough, olive-green wool of Frosty's new uniform. "You are so dear to me, my Alice." Frosty whispered. She grasped his coat hoping to hang onto him. But his buddies jostled forward and swept him towards the waiting train. She flashed her much-practiced smile and he was gone.

Her last glimpse of the boys was on the train. All five struggled for space at the narrow window, their bulky hats comically fighting as they leaned out, grinning. Alice caught Frosty's eye. Jumping up over the crowd she waved. His head ducked back in. All she could see as the train pulled away was his hand, stretched out the window, waving goodbye.

*Alice and Martin at Ansfred's, East of Wenona for dinner.
Before Martin enlisted to go to war.*

Chapter

19

Excerpts from Frosty's actual letters home.

March 6, 1918, Fort Leavenworth

Dear Alice,

It's real Kansas weather here, Al. We were issued a uniform and reported at 8:00 a.m. for special duty. Now my surname and address is Carl M. Appleton Co. B, 3rd Depot Battalion, Signal Corps, Fort Leavenworth, Kansas. I got a perfect fit in uniform which others or some didn't, so now I'm a real soldier, believe me. Today we filled our bed ticks with straw from the barn. We are all in the same barracks so far, all fourteen of us. There are 85 sleeping in one room, all in white single iron beds. For a person that hasn't seen a camp, it surely would be great to visit. I am going to send my clothes home today. I am now awaiting inspection. Think we will be here for at least six months. My first vaccination did not take so I had to go over again the whole thing. I sure feel it in my arm this time, so it must be taking.

I received the box and everything in it. Many thanks, but it costs too much to send it. It was great to get. Sergeant said he would have to inspect it, so I gave him a piece of my cake. I feel sorry for those who have no one at home to write to them.

March, 1918, Fort Leavenworth

Received your letter yesterday and was real glad to get it. Am a little tired at night now, because we sure do get some real work, believe me. Had a ten mile hike last Friday forenoon. We were on the road three hours. The farmers were all out in the fields working and the dust flying so it made me little homesick to see them disking and harrowing. After we got back we all had our feet examined.

Was to church twice yesterday, so am getting real good. There are eighteen churches here so you see it isn't a very small town. Seven of us walked down into church and took dinner downtown and then walked back. Certainly was a treat to eat where there was a tablecloth and something different to eat.

Have seen some real Kansas whirlwinds already and believe me they are a fright. Had one today when we were out drilling. I will now try to give you a little idea of what we do here. We get up at 5:45, revele at 6:00, breakfast at 6:15. Then clean house until 7:30, take out all beds, sweep and scrub. Drill from 7:30 until 8:30. Physical exercise from 8:30 until 9:30. Telegraphy from 9:30 until 10:30 and flag signaling from 10:30 until 11:30 and dinner at 12:00. Afternoon starts at 1:00 and same thing over. We are done a little earlier here than on the farm. At 5:00 is retreat. Everybody stands up and faces the sun, answers roll call and salutes while the band plays the Star Spangled Banner.

Today we were on parade. Believe me that was a beautiful sight. Every soldier marching with time to the band. They have a real band to play all the time. Alphonso was over before supper so we had a little talk. We were out walking last evening, him and I, down by the Missouri River and around a little. Just like the 4th of July. It is just as warm here now as in June or July in Illinois, so what will it be this summer with felt hats? Well, the Germans certainly are raising cain now. The soldiers don't talk much about war here. They get excited and want to go over right away. Got The Wenona Index yesterday. I read it about 25 times, so I know it all by heart.

You were wondering what I was doing on my birthday, well,

I will tell you. I was working in the kitchen all day, from 5:30 a.m. until 6:30 or 7:00 at night. There is a Norwegian in our barracks here that sure is a card. We sing together and we have the whole bunch laughing. This sure is the liveliest bunch of kids here I have ever seen in my life. A person can laugh until he cries. Our bunch just sent for five dollars worth of candy, so that will last a few days anyway. Well, it's nine o'clock now, so the lights will soon go out. Am getting sleepy so will close for this time.

Love to all, Martin

March 28, 1918, Fort Leavenworth, Kansas,

The weather certainly is changeable. Funny there aren't more sick than there are, but I guess everybody has the Kansas Hack, as they call it. Days are awful hot, and nights turn colder than blazes. We were issued another blanket, so now we have three. We sleep with our sweaters and overcoats on too. Have a headache quite a bit.

Tomorrow we go on a long hike again. It isn't bad for me, because I am used to walking, but it goes pretty tough on some of them. Everybody seems to enjoy it though, because they can sing and smoke and believe me, they do sing. We rest twice, and everybody sits down on the side of the road. We got our full equipment day before yesterday so now we have more stuff to tend to. We take them on our backs when we go on a hike. They weigh about sixty pounds. Sunday is Easter, and am going to church if I am all right. One consolation, I don't need to buy a suit or hat for Easter.

In one house between town and the Fort here, there are five gone from one family. They have a large service flag and five big stars on it. I will have to close for this time, as it is nearing one o'clock and then is when the grind starts again. Write soon, Lovingly, Martin

Post Hospital, Diphtheria Unit, Fort Leavenworth

Didn't have a very good night last night. Haven't been up today so I am trying to scribble a few lines in bed. Pretty cold here today, so it feels good to be under the blankets. Another diphtheria case came in our room today, but it is lonesome anyway. This new fellow is getting his shot in the belly now, so can you hear him squeal? It makes you jump all right. I was just looking into his face and he was grinning and gritting his teeth for all he was worth. How are the men getting along in the field? Suppose they are working early and late as usual.
Love to all, Martin

Post Hospital, Fort Leavenworth, April 22, 1918
Dear Folks,

Just received your letters and was certainly glad to get them. Am getting stronger every day. I've been up here two weeks today and it seems like two years, and I don't know if I will be out in two more weeks or not. Have been getting real cranky and tough – so if I stay up here another week everybody will be scared of me. The greatest guy I am going to miss up here is a Chinese kid. He isn't really from China, but can talk Chinese. He certainly is a fellow full of fun. Have a very sick man across the hall. I don't know what is the matter with him, but he isn't expected to live.

You can't see my face for whiskers and hair. I sure will look like something when I get out of here. I suppose everybody is busy around there these days. How do you like the hired man, and can he work? I suppose if I went to hitch up a team I would put them both on the same side of the tongue. How is the old Ford holding out? Wish I had it out here, and I would see how many telephone posts I could take down. Got the box you sent with tobacco, soap, cookies, cigars and Nabiscos – thanks for it.

Gee, you must have been awful scared about that suitcase I sent. I sent it two weeks before I got sick, so I guess there weren't any germs in it. One of the boys in my room got a cake in the mail yesterday, but it didn't last long. Alice sent me this writing paper so that's why I am so sporty today. Will be busy writing all day today, I suppose, but that's all we can do. Don't worry about me, 'cause I am doing fine.

Love to all, Martin

Post Hospital, Fort Leavenworth, Kansas, May 8, 1918

Am just crazy to get out of here. I bet if I ever will get out, I will jump over trees, telephone wires and everything. Been up in the window looking at a funeral. He died with scarlet fever. I believe it was the biggest funeral I have ever seen. A military funeral is awful sad. The band always plays and marches in front of the corpse. Sunday was a swell day, and there are thousands of people out here just walking around. I just kept running from one window to another watching them. I still have one partner here yet, as he didn't get out last week as was expected. Was outside yesterday on the porch and had a sunbath. First time I have been outside since I got here. Got pretty weak then, believe me.

That tobacco you sent me got up here, so I sent for a cob pipe and that's about my best friend here. Gee, the way I puff on that thing sometimes, you'd think the hospital is on fire. It is furlough now, and what I wouldn't give for a cup of mother's coffee and sinkers [donuts]. Gee, that makes my stomach holler worse when I think about it. When I was out on the porch, I was talking to a fellow that has been in the hospital over three months. If I stay that long, I think I will croak. Don't worry about me, 'cause I am doing fine.

Martin

At Heflin's store, customers streamed in the front door on the first warm day of Spring. "It's such gorgeous weather today," Alice said to Jenny, "I thought I'd wear my prettiest white dress. Now look at it!"

"You can tell you've been pulling dirty hat boxes down from the shelves," Jenny replied. "They have been gathering dust all winter. But now, thanks to your white dress, it looks like they're all properly cleaned off!"

"Happy to help," Alice said with a wry smile and a curtsy. Then the front door jingled and once again consumed with families purchasing fabric for spring dresses, light leather shoes to replace their heavy winter boots and fresh new linens to freshen to spruce up musty rooms.

It was almost closing time. The girls leaned on the counter, waiting to count the money and close the till. "My feet are so sore," Jenny said. "I feel like I haven't sat down all day."

"Me too," Alice replied, dabbing at the dirtiest spots of her dress with a wet rag. "I'm looking forward to parking myself on the porch swing and resting these tired toes."

The front door bell jingled again and the girls silently groaned, one last customer. Alice looked up to see all the girls staring at the door. "What?" she asked in response to Jenny's stunned gaze. A dark figure stood silhouetted in the bright glass. Alice's knees felt weak. For a brief minute, her eyes seem to lose focus. It was like seeing a ghost. Softly she said, "Frosty?"

"I thought for a minute you didn't recognize me, Al," he replied with a crooked smile. He rushed towards her and scooped her into a fierce hug. Her tired feet dangled in the air, lighter than leaves.

"It's really you!" Alice cried.

Frosty set her down on the hardwood floor. "Yes, it's

me in the flesh. Thought I'd come over and buy my best gal an ice cream."

"What's all the commotion?" Mr. Heflin asked, coming out of the back room. "Well, Frosty, what a surprise! Are you back for awhile?"

"A ten-day furlough, sir."

"That's wonderful! I heard you were sick."

"Yep, diphtheria. I was at the Post Hospital for weeks. Can't tell you how great it feels to be out." He smiled warmly at Alice. "Or how great it feels to be home."

"I can only imagine," Mr. Heflin said. "Hey, you two, how about I take your picture to commerate this grand occasion? I'll grab my Kodak and we'll go out back."

Standing in the warm sunshine with Frosty beside her, Alice could hardly believe this day. Smiling for the camera was no problem at all.

That night, dinner at the Appleton's was a celebration. Mrs. Appleton prepared all of Frosty's favorites and everyone teased him about his amazing appetite. "Go ahead and laugh," Frosty mumbled good-naturedly, his mouth full of lemon pie. "I haven't eaten this good in months."

"Be careful or you won't fit into your uniform ten days from now," Mr. Appleton joked. "You won't look nearly as smart with the buttons popping off of that shirt!"

"I'll take my chances," Frosty said. "Delicious pie, Ma. I could go for another piece."

Mrs. Appleton playfully slapped Frosty with a napkin. "Let that poor belly of yours have a break. Go on outside and sit with Alice a bit while I clean up the kitchen."

With an exaggerated groan, Frosty rose from the table, hunched over and held his stomach. "Help me to the swing, Al," he moaned. "And mind you don't go too fast!"

It was a beautiful night. "I told the girls I was planning

to sit on the swing tonight and rest my poor feet," Alice said. "But I never imagined I'd be swinging with you!"

"Life sure takes some twists and turns, doesn't it Al? I've been lying in that hospital bed, watching everyone ship off but me. I wasn't sure I'd ever get out of that room, much less over to Germany. And here they up and surprised me with a furlough trip home! That was the last thing I expected."

"It's amazing," Alice murmured, "Ten days! We'll be able to go to the band concert and maybe out for a picnic. I think I'll ask Mr. Heflin if I can have a little time off, and we can ..."

"Whoa!" Frosty said, laughing. "I need to help out while I'm here. Pa really had to pick up the slack with Paul and I both gone."

"You're right," Alice conceded. She squeezed his arm. "It's just great having you back."

Before he could reply, Frosty and Alice heard the noisy crunching of car tires coming down the gravel road. Headlights split through the dark. "Now who could that be?" Frosty said. They stood together to get a better look.

The family came out of the house and crowded on the porch. Mrs. Appleton wiped her hands on a dishcloth, her eyebrows crinkled, her lips tight. She's worried, Al thought with surprise. She glanced at Mr. Appleton. His mouth tugged anxiously on this pipe. Alice slipped her hand into Frosty's and he smiled. "A late night well-wisher, no doubt. I hope they're not expecting pie!" he chuckled.

The dusty auto came to a halt. Frank from the post office stepped into the headlight's glare. He shuffled his feet and noisily cleared his throat. "A telegram came for you Frosty. Thought I needed to bring it out right away."

Frosty's smile faded as he stepped up to Frank's out-stretched hand. Alice felt his warm fingers slip from hers. Frosty stood in the harsh lights, ghostly again.

"They need me back," Frosty's voice echoed as if from a thousand miles away. "I leave on the train tomorrow at sunrise."

Alice and Frosty behind Heflin's store on his short furlough.

Chapter

20

Excerpts from Frosty's actual letters home.

Friday Afternoon, Fort Leavenworth, Kansas

We are just waiting to go. Got everything ready. Could tell you where but don't dare. Two of our boys got turned out so they don't get to go with us. Will get out late tonight or early tomorrow morning. The boys can't leave camp so there are lots of people and girls visiting. Am pretty tired because I have been working hard every minute since I got back. We might get a chance to drop a line or two on the way, but I doubt it, so you probably won't hear from me for a spell.
Love to all, Martin

May 29, 1918, Camp Mills, Hempstead NY,

The trip out here from Kansas was 2,200 miles. That was the fastest train ride I have ever had, and the best. The people go wild when a troop train goes through. I could hardly talk when I got here, and my arm was all sore. I suppose Alphonso is lonesome now, but one of the Henry boys got left too, so it won't be so bad. The rest are all still together and we see each other every day. One buddy went to New York today, but he only got a twelve-hour pass. He is having trouble with his ears and Browning is in the hospital now, so suppose he will get left behind too.

It is great to see the airships here. They are as thick as hair on a bug's back and they can do some stunts, believe me. Makes me wish I were up in the air with them. Was out to Coney Island and all the high places in New York. You ought to have seen me go parading down Broadway. Just like a millionaire's son. The corn is up about a foot around here. They are plowing to beat the band. I saw the funniest thing yesterday. I saw a horse hitched up to a cart, and I bet my shoes it was Old Bill. He would step and limp, and whenever he saw a car he would stick his old head up. Just like Old Bill used to do.
Lots of Love to All, Martin

June 3, 1918, Camp Mills, Hempstead NY,
My Dear Folks,

Just imagine me sitting here in my underwear writing and trying to keep cool and keep the mosquitoes away. They nearly eat a man up out here. Got off guard duty this noon after a twenty-four hour shift. So am a little sleepy tonight. Only got three hours sleep last night and walking the rest of the time. Well, we are left behind now as our company sails tomorrow or Monday. The latest reports are that they go to Italy for awhile and then on to France. Certainly too bad we got left behind, but I guess it couldn't be helped. We have a nice bunch of fellows in my tent that got left. We'll be here for two weeks more anyway, as we have to stay in quarantine at least eighteen days and maybe more. The people have been going past today when they go to the beach, which is only three miles from here. Am going to try and get there myself before I get out of here, when I am this close. The airplanes have been hitting the tent tops all day today as they have been flying awfully low. Took a nice cold shower bath this afternoon, so I feel like a fighting bird. Got six letters all at once today, so got lots of news. Have got iron beds out here and real springs, so we sleep pretty fair, only for those pesky horse-

flies and mosquitoes. It is getting dark now, so will have to turn on my electric light, which consists of a candle. Sure do think a lot of you every day up here in New York. Didn't ever expect to see all the interesting things that I have seen. The company sure did hate to see us left behind also. About half of them cried when we said goodbye to them. The officers were a fine bunch of men. Well, the company would all get split up when they get over there anyway, so we couldn't have been together long. I think I had better quit now and hit the feathers.

Love, Martin

June 13, 1918, Camp Mills, Hempstead NY,

Will now write you a few lines. Just did my washing - a union suit, a shirt and a pair of socks. Last week I boiled my clothes and my wool shirt shrunk up to beat the band. The boys left Sunday, I guess, 'cause I haven't heard anything of them. Are some pretty seasick boys by this time waiting for the moon to come up. How are the band concerts coming along? I bet it is pretty dead alongside of what they were last summer. We are due out of here Monday or Tuesday - that is, our eighteen days are up then. They have a raft of people here. One hundred fifty came in late last night. Been having lots of rain again. It never knows when to stop in this state. Oh, for a good cup of coffee and real cream. Well, I will quit for this time hoping these lines find you well.

Love, Martin.

June 23, 1918, Camp Merrit, Jersey City, New Jersey,

This is certainly some place and has got everything beat that I have seen. Getting all our equipment again as they took all our stuff away from us when the company left us. I got two new suits of clothes and a new hat, so I look just like a professor man. Don't know if they are going to issue us any pants or not, but hope so, and then I will have some pictures taken. They certainly entertain the soldiers in this camp. They have four Y.M.C.A.s, and something doing in each one every night, besides two big Liberty Theaters and a Knights of Columbus Hall. Lots of fellows that got left in Leavenworth just came the other day and have left already. They are going to beat us across after all. Haven't had any drilling or work since I got sick, so I will be a regular recruit and a greenhorn again.

Got a new name. It is Blondie, now. Had to have my golden locks cut off today though. Everybody had to get their hair cut short. This place is packed with boys, and I am amazed to look around and see the different types of men there are in this world. A person can't realize what kind of types there are until he sees them. It seems like there's enough boys here to whip every German that ever lived. A great army left here last night and I suppose it won't be long before we get our order to pack up too. Well, there is no news here, so will close, hoping to get your letters soon.

Love, Martin

June, 1918, Wenona, Illinois,

My Dear Frosty,

I hope this letter finds its way to you. By this time you may already be out to sea. I can't imagine so many days with nothing to see but water! I hope you can keep from getting seasick - that would make for a miserable trip.

Things are fine here. It seems strange to go to church and the Wednesday night concerts and see so few men there. We have had a busy time at the store. Spring and summer fashions all feature narrow waists, which require a corset. I have become Heflin's expert on corsets and just last week I took the train over to Streator for an all day class in corset fitting. You'll notice my fancy title in the

The Wenona Index that I've enclosed. Find the ad for A.A. Heflin's, where corsets are on sale for just $3.50. "Any lady who has not secured a corset is urged to visit our corset department today and have our corsetierre, Miss Crone, fit you." How about that!

A group of ladies in Osage township have organized a Chapter of the Red Cross and I went to the first meeting at Phoenix school. So many people have turned out to help pack boxes of linens for bandages and care packages for the troops. It's hard to imagine that you'll soon be in Europe, heading for the front lines. We've read news reports of how they fight there, dug down in muddy trenches, making a quick run-for-it across no-man's land to jump into the next sloppy trench. Of course, you always were the best runner at our baseball games! You'll no doubt make it just fine. Know that I am thinking of you every minute.

Lovingly, Alice

July 7, 1918, Sunday afternoon, On Board Ship
Dear Folks,

Will now write you a few lines on board here so you will get it that much sooner if we land alright – which I hope we do. Am feeling fine now – but the first three days got my goat. Wasn't out of bunk for three days with seasickness. When I get off this boat will have to hire somebody to rock me to sleep every night as we certainly do get rocked on the boat. Today I believe is the calmest day we have had yet. Saw two other ships yesterday which was a welcome sight to see and what will it be when we sight land. The Knights of Columbus, Red Cross and Y.M.C.A. are along. Last Thursday they had a big program, but it wasn't like Fourth of July in the dear old Wenona. Haven't written a letter in so long I have almost forgotten how to write, and a fel-

low has to be careful now what he writes, 'cause they censor all the mail. Don't know how often you will hear from me, but will do the best I can.

I haven't had a decent wash or drink since I have been on board, as the water is all salt water and it makes you dirtier than you were to begin with. Have stood on guard once since I got on the boat and it is interesting to stand all night and watch out in the water. We carry our life preservers with us all the time, every step we take. We also have boat drill to our lifeboats once every day. Will drop you a few lines again when we land. Greet everybody and love to all, Martin

July, 1918, On Board Ship,
Dear Alice,

Keep up your spirit and don't weaken and that's about all that can be expected of you. It seems like I am writing my own death sentence, and it probably is. Greet all my friends and your folks and again thanking you for how dear and true you have been to me. I trust and leave you in God's hands. Most devotedly yours, yours forever, Carl Martin

First month in World War I, Frosty is front row, left.

Chapter
21

Excerpts from Frost's actual letters home.

Friday, July 12th, Somewhere in France

We are landed, and safe and sound on the ground again. This sure is some grand country and scenery, but so different from what we are used to. We are at the rest camp now, but don't know how long we will be here. They always take them here a few days to rest up after the trip is over. Had a long hike up here from the boat landing, so we were a pretty tired bunch last night, and today everybody is stiff and can hardly move. Was pretty nice to get some old white bread again. All we had on the boat was French rye bread. Have seen 20 of our old company here, but they are all split up. They are all over France. Was nice to see them, believe me. They had us reported lost when we landed, but we weren't.

If anybody says anything about hard times at home, they ought to be out here and I believe they would change their minds. Am learning French pretty good, so I can understand just a bit of it. The worst part is the money. If you buy something for a nickel in American money and give them a dime or a quarter, they give you a handful of change back.

Our barracks bags were lost coming over, so we have to get new stuff again. All my personal stuff was also lost, some of which I wouldn't have parted with for love or money. Have seen some sights already that will always remain in my mind, believe me. I will close for this time, hoping you are well.
Love to all, Martin

July 22, 1918, France,
I think I am settled in for a while. Am in a regular company again, which makes it a whole lot better. Have been traveling since landing here. Are having hot weather now, and the flies and bugs won't leave us alone. Have seen some more of my company. They are scattered all over, but suppose we will run across some wherever we go. This is a great country, but give me the good old USA for mine every day. It surely is a pity how they abuse the horses over here. They drive small burrows like Kenneth had, for great big wagons.

It seems like I move every Sunday since I enlisted. Every move I have made so far has been on a Sunday. The trouble with me here, I can't keep the days and dates straight. I never know what day it is anymore. I get them all mixed up and they are all the same. One thing we've got in this country is good road! You have to give them credit for that. Uncle Sam has taken possession of everything over here. Seems like there isn't any French here at all, but all...[cut out by the censors]...them and still coming. Well, as the bugle just blew for dinner, I think I will have to quit for this time.
Love, Martin

Wednesday, September 4, 1918, Somewhere in France,
My Dear Folks,
Don't worry about me, as I know you will especially, Mother. I sincerely hope you keep your health and have a brave heart.

Life out here is getting more entertaining every day. There are lots of interesting things that I would like to tell you about, but you know as well as I do that it wouldn't get past the censor. I hope some day to be able to tell you of this wonderful trip that anybody ought to be proud to have made and not ashamed to talk about. Where is Fred camped at now? Would be great if you could send some of the Indexes out here. Am going to ask Alice for Peddy's address so I can write to him. Would like to know where they are at and what they are doing. We had a very nice walk the other night of seven hours, but then you know that's army life. You have to grab some sleep on the run. It is very interesting to see an air battle between airplanes, but believe me it isn't interesting when they start a raid on you. A person is just like a squirrel then, he hunts for a hole. Art isn't married yet is he? I suppose he and Ansfred have to register now too. Everywhere we are, the Germans and French have been ahead of us.

Had a nice rain last night which settled the dust, which was at least six inches deep. The traveling and traffic is so great, so that is what makes it. Had a ride in a truck the other day all day. Couldn't tell you how long the train of trucks was, 'cause I suppose you wouldn't believe me. Well, I think I will close for this time, hoping these lines find you all in good health and enjoying yourselves. Greet the neighbors, and Love to all.
Martin

Wenona, September, 1918
Dear Martin,

Today is a glorious Fall day – I'm wondering what Autumn is like in France? Maybe we can go back some time for a visit after this nasty war is over. We could see the Eiffel Tower and walk along the famous River Seine. Speaking of rivers, we had a church gathering at Sandy

Creek last weekend. Timber was full of brilliant oranges and reds. I barely got to see them since my snappy new hat has a brim as wide as a barrel! Everyone is wearing them, and I've been lucky enough to spot the prettiest ones when they come into the store. Mr. Heflin is a little worried about a shortage of coats. Wool is in short supply because of the demand for uniforms and it is expensive. The most inexpensive new coat we've received is $19.75. I have to admit the one that has caught my eye sells for the scandalous price of $47.50. I will just have to settle on admiring it on display each day.

Everyone is fine here. We miss you. People are always asking me where you are stationed and offering encouragement. I visited with your parents Sunday at church and they are well. Your mother mentioned she hardly knows how much to cook anymore, with all the boys gone from the house! I hope you're eating some of that fine French cooking, though I'll bet it's not on the army's menu. I miss you and will write again soon.
Love, Alice

September, 1918

Didn't get this letter finished yesterday, so will endeavor to do so today. Had a nice rain last night, which was certainly needed on account of the roads. Am lucky enough to be in a dugout now and also to have a bunk, although you must remember it is nothing but sleeping on plain boards. It is better than sleeping on the damp ground though. Here it is already September, and it does seem like two years since I left you all, although we know that it isn't quite that long. Heard all about that accident at Peoria and it certainly was awful. You would think that was awful back in the States, but if you only knew what was taking place out here in "Sunny France" you would probably change your minds.

Don't know if I told you what I was doing or not. I am doing panel signaling to the airplanes and like it fine. Have been having an awful battle with the cootie bugs for a couple of days, but I have shown them that I am boss now. They are so big and old that they have service stripes on them!

Well, I think I will drop these lines for this time and will write a little later as time allows. Hoping these lines find you in good health and spirits. Greet your folks for me. I remain lovingly yours, Martin

Frosty.

Boys from Wenona and Henry, all enlisted in World War I.
Martin, standing far right.

First World War I boys to leave Wenona together.
Martin first row, far right.

Chapter
22

Wenona, November 11th, 1918

Dear Frosty,

It's over! I can hardly believe the Armistice has been signed. Signed on the 11th hour of the eleventh day of the eleventh month — will always remember this moment. The war is over. And now you'll soon be home! You wouldn't believe how the town celebrated when we heard the news. Before the sun was up, church bells rang out from every corner, rousting everyone out of bed. The whistle blew in the coal shaft and people began shooting off guns, banging drums and tooting horns clear before sunrise. The noise and the celebration went into the night. No one went to work and everyone turned out into the streets to hug each other and cheer. All day, boys and girls paraded through the streets, banging whatever they could find to make a big noise. Everyone was laughing and crying at the same time. Older people decorated their porches with flags and bunting. Shortly before dinner time, people gathered uptown, expecting something but not sure what. About 2:30, the Wenona Band took up in the band shelter and gave a concert. Then came a parade of the veterans

of the Civil War only seven of them joined in, followed by the Woman's Relief Corps and Miners' Union. All types of townspeople, men, women and children. The parade halted in front of the band shelter, and then such a sight. Several men came out carrying a dummy of the German Kaiser, which they hung on a wire over the street. A firing squad, at the officer's command, the Kaiser's body reiddled with shot and it fell to the street with a thud. Mayor Grants made a speech, as well as our Reverend Hamilton and many of the other ministers in town. Everyone carried on far into the night. Armistice! It has a wonderful ring to it! Finally, I'll see you home soon, Martin.
Love, Alice

Thursday, November 14, 1918, Somewhere in France

Will write you a few lines tonight, and I believe it is the happiest letter I have written yet. We have at last shown them what the Yankee boys can do, and I am a pretty tickled boy. Believe me, I am not the only one. It is just like entering a new life now. We are in the front lines again, so I have a fair notion that I will see the Rhine, and I sure would love to do that.

We all had a bath yesterday, which was very much needed and I feel about ten or fifteen pounds lighter. It is funny to see the cars and trucks going around with lights on and everything else lit up. They shoot skyrockets at night so it reminds one of the 4th of July. It certainly does seem funny not to hear the rumble of the guns any more, and the other day how suddenly they stopped at eleven o'clock. Believe me, we are having some cold and Frosty weather now. Hoping to hear from you soon,
Love, Martin.

Monday, November 25, 1918, Somewhere in Luxemberg

Just a few lines to let you know that I am still well and happy as ever. Am still on my way and this is a trip I wouldn't have minded for anything in the world, although it is hard work. Have been on the trip just a week now and have still got about ten days travel ahead of us before we get to our destination. I must tell you that I had French waffles the other day, the first I have had since I left home, and I ate eight large ones. Can you imagine that? But everything costs like the dickens here, so a person has to go a little easy. The people back in the states talk of hard times and high prices, but if they lived over here awhile they would have seven kinds of fits. One hundred dollars for a sack of sugar, and meat at $1.25 a pound. What I wouldn't give now for about twenty buckwheat cakes and some good old country sausage. Well, I have had French meals and German meals already, but none of them taste as good as the old American meals. The Germans can make pretty good coffee though, I will say that much for them. I'll close now for this time, as its getting close to dinner time, at least my stomach feels that way. Love, Martin

Tuesday, December 19, 1918, Sayn, Germany, Army of Occupation

We arrived at this place last Friday the 13th, an unlucky day, but we didn't fall into the river when we crossed it either. We crossed the Rhine at 7:15 in the morning. It is some long and fine bridge that we crossed. I just finished taking a bath this afternoon so I feel like a newborn babe, and so light I can hardly stay on the ground. I weighed myself last night, but then I had all the dirt and dirty clothes on yet, so that is why I weighed so much I guess. I weighted 185 pounds; can you imagine that? Next thing to do is find somebody to wash my dirty clothes, as it would take me a whole week to get them clean, but then I have only had them on a little over five weeks so its not so bad.

Well, this has been a wonderful trip and if they would have

*offered to send me back home an hour after the armistice was
signed, I believe I would have turned it down. But then don't
take it for granted that it was a trip of fun or luxury, 'cause
believe me, it wasn't. The people over here all wonder why we
carry our guns all the time, as we can't step outside at all without our guns with us. I slept in a real bed last night, but wasn't
content, and couldn't sleep at all. I would sooner take my blankets and sleep on the floor. These beds are just like the French
beds. A person has to have a ladder to get in them, or else take
a long run and jump in. The people have treated us better than
the French did. This place here is an old historic place. I was in
a castle the other day that was over seven hundred years old. It
is right in the valley with mountains all around it, so it makes
nice scenery when a person is up and looks down. The people
are plowing here now. They're out in the fields driving a couple
of steers or oxen, as the horses are scarce. It is only seven days
away from Christmas, and I can hardly realize that I am so far
from home. Hope I will be there next year to spend Christmas.
Love to all, Martin*

December 31, 1918, Rengsdof, Germany,
My Dear Folks and All,

*Received three letters from you and mother's card and mon-
ey order. Many thanks, dear mother, and rest assured that you
have always been in my thoughts the past year. Have still got a
five dollar bill that I have had from the states, and am certainly
going to take it back with me, if I go, which I hope to do. Yesterday was Monday, and my wash day. I did it myself and must
say I did a great job. Surprised myself, as I had the underwear
on six weeks, but they are as white as this paper now, and I bet
there isn't a cootie on them. But then, it doesn't make any dif-
ference, they will be there in no time. I laughed the other night
reading one of your letters. You said, "good night and don't let*

the cooties bite." Well, just then there was one biting on my back to beat the band. A person has to turn them over, but that doesn't do any good either 'cause they got legs on both sides. Must tell you I had a German shave the other day and it will be my last one, too. It costs about four cents to get shaved here.

This is the grandest day I have seen for about six weeks. The sun is out and shining. I have my blankets out hanging and airing out and believe me they sure need it. Tonight is the big night at home and I sure wish I was there with you – but hope I will be there next New Years! Have been over here over six months already, so now I am the proud wearer of a gold service stripe. Had a nice Xmas dinner yesterday, and I had my fill. Roast chicken, dressing, roast pork, mashed potatoes, gravy, apple pie, bread, butter and coffee. We had to travel in the truck fifteen kilometers to the company, as they are not where I am. There isn't room in this town for Division Headquarters and the Signal Corp also. I haven't been with the company now for about three months. Night before Xmas, two Germans came into town with each a deer over their shoulder. Looked mighty nice, believe me.

So Carl and Eva already have a squawker. I bet it seems funny to see Eva carrying a youngster around. Suppose all the corn is out of the field now, or close to at least. Well, corn husking isn't so bad after all. A person is pretty mighty sure he is going to get three square meals a day and a place to sleep at nights.

Am going to tell you something funny, and you may not believe it, but it is the actual truth. Just as true as I am over here in Germany. I have slept with hogs. Right in the same pen with them. Why, if anybody could do that in the states they would shoot him or send him to Leavenworth. The hens are cackling down below and I wish that I had about a dozen of their eggs! You said you weren't going to give me any kropkaka when I get home. I think you'll have to – and the pie and cake and home-

made bread and everything else!

Lost one of my friends the other day. He was wounded in the last battle we were in. He was a Swede and his name was Lextrum. Another Swede got hit with the same shell but died instantly. His name was Strand. They sure were two nice boys. Lextrum has a brother in our company too. Hoping these lines find you all in the best of health.
Love to all, Martin

Sunday, January 12, 1919, Rengsdorf Germany,
Dear Folks and All,

Received my Christmas box o.k., and it certainly was great. Many, many thanks for it. Everything in it was just what I wanted and needed. And oh, that cake, it was almost hot yet! I bet that I can eat five big ones at least. I just got started though, and it was all gone, and I know no one took it away from me, and the same with the Hershey bars. Gee, if I ever wear these white socks, you sent, I will never get them clean.

Got an Index from Al and it was the one with Peddy's letter in it that he had written the day after the Armistice was signed. It certainly was good all right, and they sure had some celebration, but I guess they did all over. Would like to have been in Chicago or New York that day. They are cooking dinner downstairs here. Smells pretty good and I think I will invite myself down.

Got paid the other day in German money, so now I have three kinds of money. That is just as bad if not worse than the French stuff. There is nothing like the good old greenbacks of Uncle Sam. There is so much talk about when we go, but I'm not paying any attention to it at all. If we are home by fall, I think I will be lucky. Accidents will happen though. I wish that the sun would just shine one day here so I could see what it looks like. I am afraid I would get scared and beat it.

Well, I think I will quit now, as I want to write a few lines to

Al too. Or she will think that I am running away with a little fat German girl. They all have too big feet. Hope to hear from you soon.
Love to all, Martin

January 12, 1919, Rengsdorf Germany, Sunday,
My Darling Alice,

As this is Sunday, I think it is generally a letter writing day. Received the Christmas box, and many, many thanks for your trouble and the long, weary hours spent knitting those socks! They sure are dandy. Guess I will have to hide them or sleep on them 'cause everybody envies me and the socks. I would like to have about a bushel of that fruitcake that was in the box. That sure was great and it melted right in your mouth. You said Peddy had asked Perle if she wanted to meet him in New York. That, to my estimation is something out of reason, cause he won't know when he will land or where, as there are more landing places than New York, you know, and how long will he stay there?

Are you going to have fried chicken for dinner today? Better go out and get a couple more of them 'cause I am coming down for dinner. Ha ha. Am trying to keep clean, now, and I don't want to boast, but I think I have gotten rid of the cooties. At least I haven't felt them biting for the last half-hour. I do wish one thing and that is there was some place here to hear a sermon. Haven't heard a preaching since we were back in Johnville. Gosh, I'll go to church every Sunday when I get home. Maybe… I suppose Fred is home now raising cain already, or did he get started on his way over here? Would like to run across him over here in Germany. We sure would have some time. Well, Al, I think I will draw this to a close for this time, hoping you are well as this leaves me feeling fine.
Lovingly yours, Martin

Wednesday, February 12, 1919, Rengsdorf, Germany,

Got a letter from Paul last week and he seemed bright and happy, only like the rest of us, he is ready to go home. I turned down a seven-day pass to France yesterday, 'cause I didn't care about going and then I was afraid that I might get left. This Swede boy in my company leaves to mourn on a seven day pass to France to visit his brother's grave, so I let him have my money to go on, 'cause of course he didn't have enough.

So Art has bought sheep now? Well, there will be kind of a sheep ranch there, I suppose, when I get back. Gee, the Y.M.C.A. is getting good to us now. Yesterday, they gave us free of charge imagine it, two cigars, two cans of tobacco, a pack of cigarettes, a bar of chocolate and a pack of gum a piece.

Am enclosing a couple of pages of pictures of the famous Red Arrow Division, of which I am proud to be one of its thirty thousand. They are some of the thousands of pictures of the 32nd Division on its wanderings. I picked out what I thought would be the best and most interesting, as I was either there or close to these places. Sometimes too close to suit me.

There are some dissatisfied soldiers over here, the way things are running back in the states. And now we see where they are not going to let us wear our service stripes. I sure would like to tell some of those guys what I think of them. Will close now, with lots of love to you all,
Martin

1919, Envelope imprinted with: American Expeditionary Forces; Young Men's Christian Association, Army of Occupation

Am feeling pretty fine at present but been having trouble with my teeth again. I guess you know how I look with a big jaw. I had three pulled and gee I suffered more that day than during the whole war almost. Have heard some fine news the *last couple of days that we are soon going home and I hope it's right. So I might be home to spend the 4th of July yet and maybe earlier. I hope so. Actually today is the first day I believe that I have been very homesick since I left home. Everybody talks now of going home and that's all you hear, so that makes it worse. I had a letter from Peddy and one from Fred Kuehn the same day as one from home and yours, and two Indexes. Everything is nothing but ice around here so you got to watch your step or you are liable to take a ride.*

We have been out maneuvering today all day but don't suppose you will know what that means so it will have to wait until I get there. It has been pretty cold today too, so I am chilled clear through and was without dinner. My nose and hands are sore, so the luckiest thing I did was when I took a jar of Mentholadum along with me. I saw in the paper tonight that the Illinois soldiers are going to get six months pay when they get mustered out. That sounds pretty good and I hope it's true. The boys here now are all getting tired and believe me they are ready to go home and I don't blame them a bit. Have got some more toothache tonight as they got cold today, so will have to go to bed early and to sleep tonight. Hoping to hear from you soon.
Love, Martin

Tuesday, February 25, 1919, Rengsdorf, Germany

I had a great boat ride on the Rhine last Saturday of about 75 or 80 miles. Talk about your wonderful scenery. Words cannot describe it. My friend got back yesterday from France where he went to see his brother's grave. He found the place all right. My pass to Paris starts next Saturday, March 1, so I look forward to a wonderful time.

The Signal Corps officers are having a great time tonight as it is the Colonel's birthday today and believe me they are going to have some feed. Two turkeys came from Paris today, and ice cream. They made pies and cakes galore. Gosh, my mouth does water. He was made Colonel about a week ago, and he is sure some man. He owns the motor car, so he has piles of money. Will close these few lines now, hoping you are all well and happy and they leave me feeling just fine. Love, Martin

Tuesday, March 11, 1919 Rengsdorf, Germany

My Paris trip came and went, and I am back again in Germany after being away nine days. I will not try and write about it, but will say it certainly is a wonderful place. Hope I will be home with you in two or three months and then I can tell you all about it. I ran across a friend in Paris that was in my company back in the states. He was surprised to see me, and of course I was the same. He and I saw New York together, but we could not see Paris together as he left the same night I got there. It was great to get to a place where you could eat what you wanted and believe me, I filled up. I wanted to get everyone something from Paris so bad, but as I left a day or two before payday, I couldn't very well do it. Every night brings us a day closer to home. Paul said he didn't know when he was going home either, but then nobody knows that and it's a good thing we don't. I had a letter from Alphonso the other day and he is the same old kid. Hoping to hear from you soon. With bushels of love, yours, Martin

Wenona, Illinois, March, 1919

Dear Martin,

I'm writing on the train, on my way home from a glorious trip to Chicago! I know you have seen such grand places, but this was a first for me and what an exciting trip it has been! I had mentioned before that Alice and Elmer Nelson had invited me to visit. Remember that they used to live in Wenona? Mr. Heflin said taking a little time off was no problem, so I took the train up a week ago. They live in a very neat brick home beside an apartment building, with a tidy little front yard. We took a picnic to the shores of Lake Michigan. I wasn't tempted to dip my toes in the water - it was freezing! We visited downtown and Alice and I shopped in the fancy stores on Michigan Avenue. Frosty, they invited me to come live with them and help with the children until I found a job and my own place to live. How about that, a farm girl like me living in the big city? What a great chance for me.

I admit that the rhythm of the train is lulling me to sleep, so I had better close for now. The Nelson's send their love, as I do.

I miss you, Alice.

Tuesday, March 18, 1919, Rengsforf Germany,

Last Saturday or March 15th was a big day for the 32nd Division. We passed in review and inspection by General Pershing. He is a wonderful man and it was a great day for us all. It sure makes some fine scene with the thirty thousand soldiers all in one place with all the artillery, machine guns and tractors, tanks and etc. We went in trucks about 25 kilometers and got back at 8:30 in the evening. You can very well imagine how hungry we were when we got home, being without dinner and then standing around all day. But then I wouldn't have missed it for anything.

The boys are rolling back to Wenona pretty fast now, and they will be coming back one by one I suppose until they are all home. Yes, I can smell those cookies cooking that you made the other day. I just wonder if I could get on the outside of six dozen like you said I could have. I don't know what to say about coming home or when, but I think I will be home in June sometime unless something unexplained happens.

I bought me a pair of shoes in Paris when I was there and last Sunday being a swell day, I put them on and paraded up and down the street. You ought to see everybody rubber-neck at me. I even had the officers looking at me.

Art sure is having tough luck with his sheep and it sure makes a person provoked then when he tries something new and it's a failure.

Am sending some paper money home, which you can have as souvenirs. Of course I cannot send the silver, so will have to carry them home. I have got a silver German dollar and one French. The German dollar is very scarce and have been offered five times more than its worth but will keep it. Will close for this time, Love, Martin.

Rengsdorf, Germany, Thursday, March 27, 1919

Gee, all we do now is stand inspections one after the other like we did at Camp Merritt before we came over here. Clothing and cootie inspections. So don't be surprised when I get home if I pull off my shirt about a dozen times a day. I sure do wish we were at our embarkation point, 'cause I do hate that trip back through France in those box cars, packed in like sardines. At first it was said we were to sail from a German port, but then there were too many floating mines, and we might have gotten blown up yet before we got there.

I was in Cologne yesterday for the day. The Germans are just as bad if not worse than the French to stick American soldiers, and they sure did it, but I did buy some things. Every window has souvenirs in them, even the butcher shops.

I saw in the paper the other day where the bill about paying the Illinois soldiers didn't pass. You have probably gotten the picture of Peter Horter, my buddy here. He is from Chicago, and he said he didn't know what he was going to do now that it didn't pass. He says he will be out of a job when he gets mus-

tered out. He is a great kid. He sleeps with his cap on and has for three years! He had his fortune told once and it was that he was going to have bad luck if he didn't sleep with his cap on for five years. So he has two more years to go.
With love to all, Martin

April 6, 1919, Rengsdorf, Germany,

We are busy every day turning in our stuff, so I think we are at last going to go home. Gee, I can see the Statue of Liberty already. I had a fifteen day pass to start today, but much to my sorrow all passes are cancelled so that means I am all out of luck.

I suppose the men are busy in the fields now by this time. I had a letter from Paul yesterday, and he said they are quarantined for measles. Well, I know what quarantine is. Just a year ago today I went to the hospital at Fort Leavenworth and spent six long weeks there and then at Camp Mills also. Know that I am on my way to old Wenona, so don't worry about anything.
Love, Martin

Friday evening, April 11, 1919, Rengsdorf, Germany,

I sent home a box the other day with my Dutch belt in it and I hope it gets there, 'cause I hear they were going to take them away from us. I didn't want to lose that 'cause I took that off of a dead, nice, big fat Dutchman and I have worn it ever since.

They have two little goats here where I live. They all keep goats here and use goat milk. I am smoking a real, honest to goodness American cigar. Can you smell it? If you smoke the Dutch smokes you either have to sit down or lay down, or else they will knock you down. The farmers are busy here now, but it sure is a joke the way they farm. If they saw the way we farm, they would fall over. The women have to be along to do everything, just like it is in France. Well, I will quit for this time,

Alice visiting Chicago, at Alice and Elmer's.

Chapter 23

Frosty had been home for days but Alice still couldn't believe it. Today he hopped off his horse in front of Aunt Tildy's and jumped the porch steps two at a time.

"Why are you looking at me like that?" he asked, amused.

"Like what?"

"Like you're looking at a ghost," he said, chuckling.

"Because I can't believe you're actually home!"

"Well, ma'am," Frosty said, sweeping into a low bow. "At your service for as long as you'll have me."

Taking Alice by the arm, he turned towards the street. "I guess we'll be walking to the picnic at the park today, since the buggy is being repaired. I don't think we want to crowd onto Old Bess." He patted the horse's muzzle as they passed.

"You're right about that." Alice said. "Besides, it's a fine day to walk." The trees were heavy with summer green and the lawns bright with recent rain.

"Oh, Frosty," Alice said suddenly. "I finished sewing your service patches onto a pillow. I meant to show you at Aunt Tildy's."

Frosty's face clouded. He didn't reply.

"I'm sorry," Alice said softly. "I didn't mean to bring it up."

Frosty hadn't talked much about the war since he got home. Alice knew that he left Rengsdorf, Germany on April 20th, 1919. Easter Sunday. She had received a telegram letting her know that they were on their way. He had come by train to Brest, France, and sailed for 12 days on the U.S.S. Rhode Island. He'd landed in Boston, then waited to leave from Camp Debens. On May 20th, he finally made it to Wenona. It had been a long journey home.

"It's alright," he said. Actually, I've been meaning to tell you a story." They ducked under a low hanging branch. "Mind if we sit on this bench?"

"I wanted to bring you something special, Al. I didn't have much occasion to buy fancy things, or room to carry them home. But this is something that I knew belonged to you the minute I picked it up." Frosty dug into his pocket and revealed a jagged piece of metal about the size of a quarter. It had razor sharp edges and a dangerous point. Alice took it from his hand. His eyes appeared to gaze at something very far away.

"We were walking through a bombed-out town in France. It was deserted, with no signs of life except smoke drifting from a couple of the buildings. I felt like every sense was alive, my eyes scanning every doorway. I expected a German to jump into the street at any second. We reached the end of town with one more building to clear – the church. I was part of the first team that went through. I crept into the sanctuary and it was a devastating scene. The entire roof was gone, with dust and debris scattered all over the carved pews. A huge ceiling beam had smashed through the altar and a fire had singed an oil painting of

Jesus. I felt like the world had turned upside down. If this could happen to God's house, how could a little guy like me, from a little town like this, hope to make it home? I knelt down on one knee right there and prayed that I'd make it back. When I stood up, I noticed for the first time that my whole company was on its knees, scattered in every open spot in this tattered church. I had a powerful feeling that I would make it.

Late that afternoon, we stretched out in a field at the edge of town. I've never been as tired as I was that day, lying in that grass. I took off my helmet, hoisted my pack off to use it as a pillow and closed my eyes right away. But just as I was nodding off, as an afterthought, I put my helmet back on and pulled it over my eyes. A second later out of nowhere, a German bomber swooped in, we were sitting ducks in an open field. Shrapnel flew everywhere. This piece hit my helmet and bounced into the grass. Lots of guys in my company were not as lucky," Martin said.

"Oh, how terrible," Alice whispered.

"Yes. But even with the horror, I couldn't help being thankful that I'd been saved." Martin looked into Alice's misty eyes and smiled. "So now you know why this junky piece of metal is so special. I wanted you to have it. It means I was meant to come back."

Alice smiled. "I couldn't imagine you not coming home."

"Now here's what I've been thinking, " Frosty said, standing up and pacing in front of the bench. "I know you've considered moving to Chicago. And I know life up there would be exciting. You never imagined making your home in Wenona forever, the wife of a farmer. You know better than most how hard of a life it can be."

"Yes," Alice said, leaning forward. "Go on."

"Well, and you know that I'm working on the farm and probably will be taking it over from Pa soon."

"Yes…"

"And so that will make me a farmer."

"I see that," Alice said. "So, just what are you trying to say, Frosty?"

He stopped pacing and nearly stumbled onto one knee. "Well, I was thinking I'd ask you to reconsider your plans, and try being a farmer's wife. Er, a, my farmer's wife. Er, I mean, my wife."

Alice burst out laughing. "Frosty, are you asking me to marry you?

His face flushed pink before he could stammer a reply. "Well, yes, I am."

Alice stared into his earnest eyes. No living in Chicago, no fast trains to New York City. Back to a farm in Wenona, something she never thought she'd do. "Another house," she murmured.

"No, Al. A home. And that's something I've learned a lot about lately. Home isn't really a place."

"No? Al, 'home' is being with someone you care about."

Alice thought back on all the places she'd lived - the farm with Minnie and Bernie, Aunt Betty's and Aunt Tildy's. Houses, places, people she loved. She had been home all along.

"Frosty, I'd love to marry you," Alice said with a smile.

"Ha! Really?" Frosty hopped up and grabbed Alice's hand. "So you and me, at the farm?"

Alice's eyes sparkled. "I know I'll feel right at home."

Epilogue

Actual Passage from Alice's Writings:

"We had a silver covered book from our wedding day out home on my father's farm. We were married among Martin's parents and brother and sister, and mine, at high noon. A lovely December 8th, 1920 wedding, with a lovely dinner following. Then we dressed to leave for Iowa for a week, to Martin's sister's. Roads were rough and weather cold with some snow, but Arthur took us in his Ford to Lostant, where we got a train. We rode all night, and Charles, Minnie's husband, met us. We had a lovely honeymoon with her and her nice family for a whole week. Then we came home, riding all night on an Illinois Central, and were met by Arthur early in the morning in Wenona.

We went right out to the farm where we lived, rented, worked, and had our Glenn, Gordon and twins Greta and Rita. Our Rita only lived eight hours, so we had many not so happy days, but we were blessed and thankful for so much. We enjoyed a full life among neighbors and relatives, and happy times raising our three lovely children."

Note From The Author

Alice and Frosty lived long lives in Wenona, surviving the Great Depression and seeing their two sons off to World War II and safely home again. Their three children flourished, and each had three children of their own. Alice and Frosty's children all attended Augustana College, as did four of their grandchildren and three of their great-grandchildren. Their youngest child, Greta, and her husband Bob, live in Wenona, where, on summer nights, you can still go to the band concert and have a wonderful piece of pie.

A century after a spunky farmer's daughter began to write down her teenage hopes and dreams, her daughter, granddaughters and great-granddaughter have brought her story to life, with daughter Greta as illustrator, granddaughters Gail as author and Polly as editor, and great-granddaughter Shelby featured on the cover.